W9-CKI-148

Ethiopia

Cavendish
Square

New York

Published in 2017 by Cavendish Square Publishing, LLC
243 5th Avenue, Suite 136, New York, NY 10016
Copyright © 2017 by Cavendish Square Publishing, LLC

Third Edition

Library of Congress Cataloging-in-Publication Data

Names: Gish, Steven, 1963- | Thay, Winnie. | Latif, Zawiah Abdul. | Nevins, Debbie.
Title: Ethiopia / Steven Gish, Winnie Thay, Zawiah Abdul Latif; Debbie Nevins.
Other titles: Cultures of the world (3rd ed.)
Description: [Third edition]. | New York : Cavendish Square Publishing, 2017. |
Series: Cultures of the world | Includes bibliographical references and index.
Identifiers: LCCN 2016030325 (print) | LCCN 2016030945 (ebook) | ISBN 9781502622099 (library bound) | ISBN 9781502622112 (e-book)
Subjects: LCSH: Ethiopia--Juvenile literature.
Classification: LCC DT373 .G57 2017 (print) | LCC DT373 (ebook) | DDC 963--dc22
LC record available at https://lccn.loc.gov/2016030325

Writers: Steven Gish, Winnie Thay, Zawiah Abdul Latif; Debbie Nevins, third edition
Editorial Director, third edition: David McNamara
Editor, third edition: Debbie Nevins
Associate Art Director, third edition: Amy Greenan
Designer, third edition: Jessica Nevins
Production Coordinator, third edition: Karol Szymczuk
Cover Picture Researcher: Angela Siegel
Picture Researcher, third edition: Jessica Nevins

PICTURE CREDITS

The photographs in this book are used with the permission of: Christophe Boisvieux/Getty Images, cover; Anton_Ivanov/Shutterstock.com, 1; milosk50/Shutterstock.com, 3; Anton_Ivanov/Shutterstock.com, 5; Aleksandra H. Kossowska/Shutterstock.com, 6; Hassan Isilow/Anadolu Agency/ Getty Images, 8; Sarine Arslanian/Shutterstock.com, 9; Peteri/Shutterstock.com, 10; Ondrej Vavra/Shutterstock.com, 12; urosr/Shutterstock.com, 14; Tomas Kotouc/Shutterstock.com, 17; Dereje/Shutterstock.com, 18; Rafal Cichawa/Shutterstock.com, 19; George Steinmetz/Corbis Documentary/Getty Images, 20; SAUL LOEB/AFP/Getty Images, 22 Tim Bewer/Lonely Planet Images/Getty Images, 23; I, Ondrej Žvácek/File:Rome Stele.jpg/Wikimedia Commons, 25; Chris Hellier/Corbis/Getty Images, 27; Keystone-France/Gamma-Rapho via Getty Images, 28; Skilla1st/File:Eritrean–Ethiopian War Map 1998.png/Wikimedia Commons, 30; Keystone/Hulton Archive/Getty Images, 32; Anton_Ivanov/Shutterstock.com, 34; Minasse Wondimu Hailu/ Anadolu Agency/Getty Images, 36; Orhan Karsli/Anadolu Agency/Getty Images, 37; Minasse Wondimu Hailu/Anadolu Agency/Getty Images, 38; Minasse Wondimu Hailu/Anadolu Agency/Getty Images, 40; PEDRO UGARTE/AFP/Getty Images, 42; Kjeld Friis/Shutterstock.com, 44; demidoff/ Shutterstock.com, 46; Fabio Lamanna/Shutterstock.com, 47; Vlad Karavaev/Shutterstock.com, 48; Minasse Wondimu Hailu/Anadolu Agency/Getty Images, 50; alfotokunst/Shutterstock.com, 52; ArCaLu/Shutterstock.com, 53; Martchan/Shutterstock.com, 55; GTW/imageBROKER/Getty Images, 57; Alberto Loyo/Shutterstock.com, 58; Alberto Loyo/Shutterstock.com, 59; Hector Conesa/Shutterstock.com, 62; Ariadne Van Zandbergen/Lonely Planet Images/Getty Images, 64; demidoff/Shutterstock.com, 68; Anton_Ivanov/Shutterstock.com, 70; Philippe Lissac/GODONG/Photononstop/ Getty Images, 72; Mariusz Kluzniak /Moment/Getty Images, 74; demidoff/Shutterstock.com, 76; Mariusz Kluzniak/Moment/Getty Images, 80; Martin Gray/National Geographic/Getty Images, 81; Dereje/Shutterstock.com, 82; Minasse Wondimu Hailu/Anadolu Agency/Getty Images, 84; Frances Linzee Gordon/Lonely Planet Images/Getty Images, 85; Keystone-France/Gamma-Rapho via Getty Images, 88; Tom Cockrem/Photolibrary/Getty Images, 90; Guenter Guni/E+/Getty Images, 93; Olivier Cirendini/Lonely Planet Images/Getty Images, 94; Anton_Ivanov/Shutterstock.com, 96; Bruno Barbier/robertharding/Getty Images, 101; Nick Fox/Shutterstock.com, 103; Clive Chilvers/Shutterstock.com, 104; Dereje/Shutterstock.com, 106; John Wollwerth/Shutterstock.com, 107; Martchan/Shutterstock.com, 108; Vlad Karavaev/Shutterstock.com, 109; Keystone-France/Gamma-Keystone via Getty Images, 110; Dietmar Temps/Shutterstock.com, 112; SIMON MAINA/AFP/Getty Images, 114; Minasse Wondimu Hailu/Anadolu Agency/Getty Images, 116; Dereje/Shutterstock.com, 117; Anton_Ivanov/Shutterstock.com, 119; rweisswald/Shutterstock.com, 122; bonchan/Shutterstock.com, 123; Anton_Ivanov/Shutterstock.com, 124; Paul_Brighton/Shutterstock.com, 126; aleksandr hunta/Shutterstock.com, 127; Eran Yardeni/Shutterstock. com, 128; Fanfo/Shutterstock.com, 130; Paul_Brighton/Shutterstock.com, 131; Mr. Alien/Shutterstock.com, 137.

PRECEDING PAGE
A young man from Ethiopia.

Printed in the United States of America

CONTENTS

ETHIOPIA TODAY

ETHIOPIA IS A UNIQUE AND EXTRAORDINARY PLACE. IT'S A LAND of ancient mysteries, dramatic scenery, surprising revelations, and curious contradictions. The name *Ethiopia* derives from the Greek *aithiopia*, meaning "land of the burned [dark-skinned] faces." The ancient Greeks used this term to refer to all places south of Egypt, which was, to them, the outer edge of the known world. Ethiopia is mentioned several times in Homer's *The Iliad* and *The Odyssey*. The region is also referred to in the Bible; however the Hebrews called it Kush (or Cush). The Ethiopia of much earlier times was not bound by the same borders as today's country. In ancient texts, Nubia, Kush, and Ethiopia were kingdoms in the part of Africa that today encompasses southern Egypt, Sudan, South Sudan, Eritrea, and Ethiopia.

Some people interpret a biblical passage in Genesis as suggesting that the Garden of Eden was located in Ethiopia. Although many religious scholars disagree with that interpretation, the claim that human life began in Ethiopia is, from a scientific point of view, surprisingly accurate. Archaeologists have unearthed fossils of the earliest known members of the human family, dating back more than two million years, in

the Awash Valley of Ethiopia. In that sense, Ethiopia has the oldest human history in the world.

Indeed, the word "oldest" applies to many things about Ethiopia. It's the oldest independent nation in Africa, governed until 1974 by one of the world's oldest monarchies. It is one of the oldest Christian nations in the world, the Kingdom of Axum being possibly the first country to officially adopt Christianity as the state religion. It was in Ethiopia that three important crops originated—coffee, grain sorghum, and the castor bean. Ethiopia is also an origin point in geographical terms. It's the source of the Blue Nile, a river that meets the White Nile in Sudan to create the Nile, one of the greatest waterways on earth.

Demographically, Ethiopia is a land of great diversity. It is home to some one hundred million people, who represent about one hundred ethnic groups, speak more than seventy languages, and practice a variety of religions.

Of all African countries, Ethiopia has the most World Heritage Sites, as listed by the United Nations Educational, Scientific and Cultural Organization

(UNESCO). World Heritage Sites are natural or human-made places or structures that have been recognized as having "outstanding international value" and therefore are deserving of special protection. Among Ethiopia's nine such treasures are the lower valleys of the Awash and Omo Rivers, where the soil has revealed numerous prehistoric fossils representing important steps in human evolution. Another World Heritage Site is found in the mountains of Lalibela, where eleven monolithic rock-hewn churches have stood since the twelfth and thirteenth centuries. These early Christian stone structures remain a holy pilgrimage destination to this day.

For all its cultural and historic wealth, however, Ethiopia today is a very poor country. It is located in the Horn of Africa, which itself is a very unstable, impoverished part of the continent. Ethiopia is still recovering from a period of violent coups, famine, and poor governance in the 1980s. Although the country is largely dependent on foreign aid, the adoption of a new constitution in 1994 saw political and economic situations finally stabilize, in a slow but steady manner.

The great diversity of Ethiopia's people and languages may be a source of cultural richness, but how does such a nation stay united? In fact, one of the country's biggest problems, aside from poverty, arises from the instability caused by the various ethnic groups asserting their rights, needs, and desires—especially in far-flung regions of the country.

For example, in the Somali Regional State in eastern Ethiopia, the people have Ethiopian nationality but identify as Somalis. In this area, also called the Ogaden, the country's borders jut sharply into the nation of Somalia. Over the centuries, the boundaries between the two countries have shifted back and forth. The people are predominantly ethnic Somali Muslims and are desperately poor. Some accuse the Ethiopian government in Addis Ababa of stealing resources from their region and giving back nothing in return. A movement for self-determination for the Ogaden, led by the Ogaden National Liberation Force (ONLF), rose up in the mid-1980s. Eventually, ONLF members took up arms and began fighting for their cause, to little effect aside from loss of life. The movement accuses the government of launching brutal crackdowns against it, which have only increased the people's suffering.

Government officials, meanwhile, blame outside agitators from Eritrea with stoking the fires of dissent. Border clashes continue to erupt from time to time.

Another situation has heated up in the country's far western Gambela region. For years, Murle tribesmen from the Boma state of South Sudan have been crossing the border into Ethiopia and stealing cattle from neighboring tribes, particularly the Nuer. By tradition, Murle men can only marry when they pay a bride price of several dozen cows. In such an impoverished region, the only way to quickly acquire cows for marriage is by stealing them.

This problem points to one of the paradoxes of Ethiopia today. Addis Ababa, the nation's sprawling capital, is a modern city of high-rise architecture and distinctive blue-and-white taxis. But in other regions of this ancient land, many people are living lifestyles based on traditions and beliefs that may no longer serve current circumstances.

Nevertheless, the twenty-first century makes itself felt. In recent years, the cross-border cattle rustling frictions between the Murle and Nuer people have turned deadly. Tribesmen now carry AK-47s as well as machetes. They abduct women and children as well as cattle. They burn villages and massacre as many inhabitants as they can. In April 2016, for example, thousands of Murle militiamen from South Sudan raided thirteen Nuer villages in Ethiopia's Gambela region. They killed more than two hundred people, kidnapped more than one hundred children, and snatched some two thousand head of cattle. The scale of that attack was unprecedented. (In June 2016, after intense government negotiations, eighty of the abducted children were returned.)

In 2015, the Fragile States Index (formerly the Failed States Index) ranked Ethiopia as number 20 in the world, with number 1 being the world's least stable nation. (In 2014 and 2015, that was South Sudan.) The index, compiled annually by Fund for Peace, a Washington, DC, nonprofit organization, assesses a country's vulnerability to conflict or collapse. For years, Ethiopia has hovered around the number 20 spot on the list, some years improving a bit, other years falling backward.

A young man protects his village in the Omo Valley.

Ethiopia today is struggling to be economically independent, politically stable, and socially integrated. Does it have the potential to reclaim the greatness of its past and compete in the world economy? In 2015, the European Council on Tourism and Trade chose Ethiopia as the World's Best Tourism Destination for that year. That's certainly a promising sign. The country's rapidly growing economy is another good omen. But many forces are at work. Border wars would surely reverse the country's progress. With many factors at play, Ethiopians continue to work toward solutions that will herald in a new era of greatness for a very old nation.

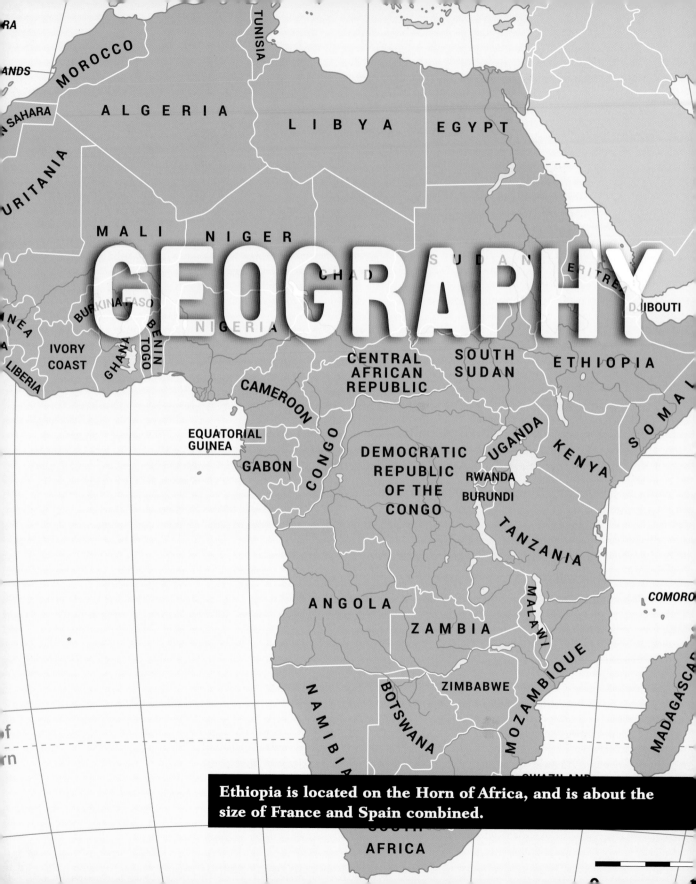

GEOGRAPHY

MOROCCO
TUNISIA
ALGERIA
LIBYA
EGYPT
N SAHARA
URITANIA
MALI
NIGER
SUDAN
CHAD
ERITREA
DJIBOUTI
NEA
BURKINA FASO
NIGERIA
BENIN
TOGO
IVORY COAST
GHANA
LIBERIA
CAMEROON
CENTRAL AFRICAN REPUBLIC
SOUTH SUDAN
ETHIOPIA
SOMALI
EQUATORIAL GUINEA
CONGO
GABON
DEMOCRATIC REPUBLIC OF THE CONGO
UGANDA
KENYA
RWANDA
BURUNDI
TANZANIA
ANGOLA
ZAMBIA
MALAWI
COMORO
NAMIBIA
BOTSWANA
ZIMBABWE
MOZAMBIQUE
MADAGASCAR
SWAZILAND
SOUTH AFRICA

Ethiopia is located on the Horn of Africa, and is about the size of France and Spain combined.

E THIOPIA IS A LARGE, LANDLOCKED country in the Horn of Africa. Located on the eastern side of the continent, the Horn of Africa is a region that juts out into the Indian Ocean. It's called a "horn" because it's a pointed protrusion, but in geographical terms, it's actually a peninsula. Some people think the peninsula resembles a rhinoceros horn. The countries of Djibouti, Eritrea, Somalia, and Ethiopia make up this region.

Directly to the north of Ethiopia lies Eritrea, which gained its independence from Ethiopia in 1993. Bordering Ethiopia to the east is Djibouti; to the south and east, Somalia; to the south, Kenya; and to the west, Sudan and South Sudan. Ethiopia lies entirely between the equator and the Tropic of Cancer. Its territory spans 435,186 square miles (1.13 million square kilometers), which is nearly three times larger than California.

Ethiopia is one of the most mountainous countries in Africa. It contains two highland regions separated by the Great Rift Valley, a vast low-lying area that divides the country roughly in half. Elevations in both highland regions can measure 7,500 feet (2,286 meters) or higher. Ethiopia's rugged terrain makes regional transportation and communication difficult, but historically, it has also protected the country from invaders.

1

Ethiopia is the most populous landlocked nation on earth, and the second most populous country on the African continent, after Nigeria.

Another key feature of Ethiopia's geography is the lack of reliable rainfall in several parts of the country. Precipitation is particularly scant in low-lying areas such as the Great Rift Valley, the Ogaden region in the southeast, and the Denakil Depression in the northeast. Droughts in these areas have caused famines throughout history. In 2016, the country faced its worst drought in fifty years, leaving 10.2 million people without food. Similar dry spells are expected to continue to plague the Ethiopian people in the future.

PEAKS AND VALLEYS

Elevation is the single most important factor defining Ethiopia's geography. It determines the climate, vegetation, soil composition, and settlement patterns of every region in the country.

Due to its mountainous terrain, Ethiopia is sometimes called "the roof of Africa." Its two major highland regions dominate the western and south central portions of the country. Rising to the west of the Great Rift Valley is the Amhara Plateau, home to the Simien and Choke mountain ranges. The elevation of these western highlands generally ranges from 7,800 to 12,000 feet (2,377 to 3,658 m) above sea level. Ras Dejen Peak, located in the Simien Mountains, is the highest point in Ethiopia, soaring to a height of 15,158 feet (4,620 m).

The Somali Plateau lies to the east of the Great Rift Valley. The Ahmar and Mendebo Mountains are found in this region. Several peaks in the Mendebo Mountains rise above 13,000 feet (3,962 m).

Valleys, deserts, and grasslands also contribute to the country's varied landscape. The Great Rift Valley cuts through much of eastern Africa and extends all the way to Mozambique in southern Africa. In Ethiopia, the Great Rift Valley ranges from 25 to 40 miles wide (40 to 64 kilometers). In the northern portion of the valley is the Denakil Depression, a desert area that lies 380 feet (116 m) below sea level. The valley's southwestern portion is dotted by a chain of freshwater and salt lakes.

LAKES AND RIVERS

The chain of lakes in the Great Rift Valley includes Lakes Abaya, Abiata, Koka, Langano, Shala, Shamo, and Zwai. Ethiopia's largest lake is Lake Tana, which lies in the northern part of the country. This freshwater lake is the source of the Blue Nile River. The Blue Nile is known to many Ethiopians as the Abbai River.

Other smaller rivers in Ethiopia include the Awash, Baro, Shebelle, and Tekeze. The government has built dams on the Awash River to generate hydroelectric power and to provide irrigation for commercial farms. Most of Ethiopia's rivers originate in highland areas and flow outward through deep gorges. This has created a series of rapids and waterfalls that, though scenic, make navigation on the rivers virtually impossible. Of all of Ethiopia's rivers, only the Awash and Baro Rivers are navigable.

A MULTITUDE OF CLIMATES

Ethiopia's varied topography and its location in Africa's tropical zone have resulted in diverse rainfall and temperature patterns. Determined to a large extent by elevation, the country's climate has three environmental zones—cool, temperate, and hot.

The highlands experience moderate to cool temperatures ranging from near-freezing to 62 degrees Fahrenheit (17 degrees Celsius), with March, April, and May being the warmest months. Lower areas of the plateau, between 4,920 to 7,872 feet (1,500 to 2,400 m) in elevation, constitute the temperate zone, where daily highs range from 59°F to 72°F (15°C to 22°C). The hospitable climate of the highland regions helps explain why they are home to the majority of Ethiopia's population. Situated in the highlands is Addis Ababa, the capital and largest city.

The Ethiopian lowlands, located chiefly in the north central and eastern portions of the country, constitute the country's hottest parts. Although the average daytime temperature is about 81°F (27°C), mid-year readings can soar from 86°F (30°C) to 120°F (49°C) in the arid and semiarid areas. Population density in the lowlands is significantly lower than it is on the plateaus.

A young girl poses on a camel in Ethiopia.

Precipitation is influenced by both elevation and season. Ethiopia receives most of its precipitation during the rainy season, which lasts from June to September. The rainy season is regarded as winter, even though it falls during the summer months, because cloud cover and rains reduce the temperature. The high plateau often gets heavy hailstorms during the rainy season, and generally receives at least 39 inches (99 centimeters) of rainfall per year. Southwestern Ethiopia receives the most abundant rainfall, an average of 56 inches (142 cm) per year.

The lowlands are much drier than the highlands and usually receive less than 19.5 inches (50 cm) of rain per year. Rainfall is particularly scant in the

ETHIOPIA'S CLIMATIC ZONES

Alpine: kur *(kuhr)*
> *Location: Ethiopia's highest elevations*
> *Elevation: Over 10,800 feet (3,292 m)*
> *Temperatures: Below 50°F (10°C)*
> *Features of interest: Regular frost; snow on highest mountain peaks. Unsuitable for agriculture.*

Cool zone: dega *(DEH-ga)*
> *Location: Chiefly northwestern (Amhara) plateau*
> *Elevation: 7,500–10,800 feet (2,286–3,292 m)*
> *Temperatures: 34°F–61°F (1°C–16°C)*
> *Features of interest: Warmest months are March to May. Light frost is common at night in the higher elevations.*

Temperate zone: weina dega *(WAY-nuh DEH-ga)*
> *Location: Lower areas of Amhara and Somali plateaus*
> *Elevation: 4,900–7,500 feet (1,493–2,286 m)*
> *Temperatures: 59°F–72°F (15°C–22°C)*

Hot zone: kolla *(KOH-la)*
> *Location: Eastern Ogaden, valleys of the Blue Nile and Tekeze Rivers, areas along Kenyan, Sudanese, and South Sudanese borders*
> *Elevation: 1,600–4,900 feet (488–1,493 m)*
> *Temperatures: Average daytime temperature is 81°F (27°C)*
> *Features of interest: The river valleys receive more rainfall than the border areas.*

Semidesert: bereha*(ber-eh-HAH)*
> *Location: Denakil Depression and other scattered, low-lying regions of Ethiopia*
> *Elevation: Below 1,600 feet (488 m)*
> *Temperatures: 86°F–120°F (30°C–49°C)*
> *Features of interest: Arid; unsuitable for agriculture.*

Great Rift Valley and the Ogaden region. Drier still is the Denakil Depression, which receives only a few inches of precipitation annually. In bad years, there is no rain at all. The Ethiopian drought of 1984 claimed the lives of nearly one million people and put eight million more on the brink of starvation. Pictures of malnourished Ethiopian children and crowded refugee camps were broadcast all over the world and triggered a massive international relief effort. (The famine is blamed on more than the drought, however. Government policies are often cited as a reason for the enormous loss of life.)

FLORA

The amount of rainfall (or lack thereof) in Ethiopia's various regions greatly affects the variety and quantity of plant life. In the driest areas, only occasional bushes and thorn scrub are found. In areas classified as semiarid, grasslands are common, as are acacia trees and sansevieria (snake plants). The cooler and wetter highlands are home to eucalyptus, yellowwood trees, and juniper.

Southwestern Ethiopia's combination of low elevation and high rainfall has produced rain forests thick with trees, ferns, and undergrowth. This unique highland ecology provided ample opportunities for Ethiopia's ancient farmers to experiment with a wide variety of crops. It is no surprise then that ancient Ethiopia was the original site of the cultivation of many food crops, including teff, which is an iron-rich grain from which the bread *injera* (in-JAIR-ah) is made. The country is probably the origin of the coffee plant as well. Today some of Ethiopia's world-famous coffee grows wild in these southwestern rain forests.

FAUNA

Ethiopia is home to an extraordinarily wide range of wildlife that in some cases have been diminished to near extinction. Foxes, jackals, wild dogs, and hyenas are commonly found throughout the country. Varieties of antelopes and monkeys are abundant in the lowlands. Elephants, giraffes, leopards, lions, rhinoceroses, and wild buffalo are rarities. Unique to Ethiopia and among the most endangered is the Walia ibex, a rare species of mountain goat that is found in the Simien Mountains. The country's lakes and rivers host crocodiles, hippopotamuses, and various other reptiles and species of fish. The Great Rift Valley is known for its bird life, which includes eagles, flamingos, and hawks. Other birds native to Ethiopia include the egret, hornbill, ibis, ostrich, pelican, stork, and vulture.

Walia ibex

A RICH URBAN HERITAGE

Although only 19.5 percent of Ethiopians live in urban areas, the cities they inhabit have long histories and compelling points of interest. Addis Ababa, the capital, has been described as a "cultural jigsaw puzzle" because of its rich mixture of peoples and lifestyles. It is also one of the largest inland cities in Africa. In 2011 the capital had an estimated population of about three million. The city is situated in the highlands at an altitude of 8,000 feet (2,438 m) and enjoys a temperate climate.

Besides serving as Ethiopia's capital, Addis Ababa is an important diplomatic center for the African continent. It is home to some ninety-seven foreign embassies and hosts international agencies such as the World Health Organization (WHO) and the United Nations Children's Fund (UNICEF). The city also serves as the headquarters for the United Nations Economic Commission for Africa and the African Union (formerly known as the Organization of African Unity, or OAU).

Ethiopia's second-largest city is Dire Dawa, which had a population of 341,000 in 2007. Dire Dawa lies between Addis Ababa and the coast and serves as an important rail terminus. In addition to Addis Ababa and Dire Dawa, Ethiopia's other important centers of trade and industry are Awassa, Gonder, Dese, Nazareth, Jima, Harer, Bahir Dar, Mekele, Debre Markos, and Nekemte.

Modern Addis Ababa began to take shape in 1889, when the Ethiopian monarch Menelik II started building a palace near the ruins of the sixteenth-century capital at Entoto. Menelik's Queen Taytu marveled at the flowering mimosa trees in the area, and thus the town was named Addis Ababa, meaning "new flower." It officially became Ethiopia's capital in 1896. Other important dates for Addis Ababa include 1958, when the city became the first headquarters of the United Nations Economic Commission for Africa, and 1963, when it hosted the African Heads of State Conference at which the OAU Charter was signed.

Among the many points of interest in Addis Ababa, two in particular stand out. One is the Giorgis Cathedral, also known as Saint George's Cathedral, which was built in 1896 to commemorate Ethiopia's victory over the Italians at the Battle of Adwa. Giorgis Cathedral features impressive stained glass created by Ethiopian artist Afewerk Tekle. Another urban wonder is the Merkato, one of Africa's largest open-air markets. Here, a dazzling array of goods is displayed for sale, including vegetables, spices, clothing, and jewelry. As it draws Ethiopians from far beyond the capital, the Merkato has been described as a melting pot for the country's different languages and cultures.

Two cities of particular historical significance are Axum and Gonder. Axum (also spelled Aksum), is located in northern Ethiopia near the Eritrean border. It was the capital of ancient Ethiopia, or the Kingdom of Aksum. Two thousand years ago, this holy city was on par with the great urban centers of Nubia, Egypt, and Greece. Axum is home to the Saint Mary of Zion Church, built in the sixteenth and seventeenth centuries and considered to be the holiest shrine in Ethiopia. Axum is also noted for its huge granite sculptures known as obelisks, some of which were over 75 feet (23 m) tall. Most of them have since fallen to the ground. Gonder, located just north of Lake Tana, served as the Ethiopian capital between 1632 and 1868. Today some of its surviving castles are used as government office buildings.

The emperor Fasilides' castle in Gonder is one of several buildings in the Royal Enclosure, a seventeenth-century fortress compound that is now a UNESCO World Heritage Site.

INTERNET LINKS

www.ethiopia.gov.et/geography
This site provides basic geography information from the Ethiopian government portal.

www.our-africa.org/ethiopia
This site has sections about many Ethiopian topics, including geography and wildlife, climate and agriculture, with videos and maps.

travel.nationalgeographic.com/travel/countries/ethiopia-guide
This site has links to a number of *National Geographic* articles and slideshows relating to Ethiopia.

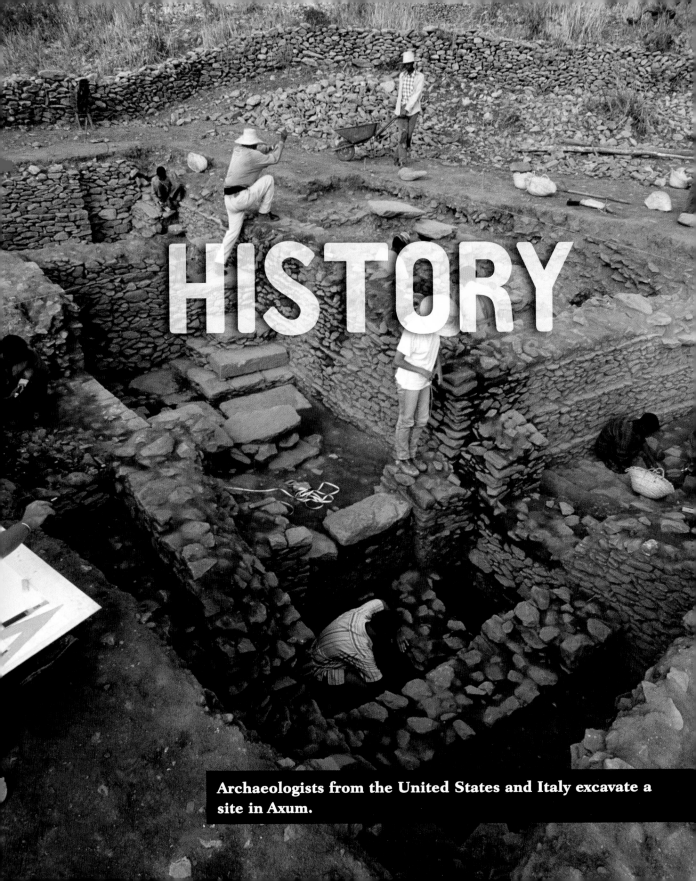

HISTORY

Archaeologists from the United States and Italy excavate a site in Axum.

2

ETHIOPIA HAS A LONGER HISTORY than almost any other nation on earth. The story of human life itself begins in east Africa, and for that reason, the region is sometimes called the Birthplace of Humankind. The oldest human fossil ever found, dating to 2.8 million years ago, was discovered in the Afar region of Ethiopia in 2013. The fossilized jawbone, identified as LD 350-1, was unearthed just a dozen miles from the location where Lucy, possibly the most famous prehuman skeleton fossil, was discovered in 1974.

That distinction alone makes Ethiopia unique among nations, but there are other particular characteristics as well. One is Ethiopia's early embrace of Christianity—it was probably the first nation on earth to accept the Christian faith. It adopted an early form of the religion more than one thousand years before European missionaries spread Christianity throughout the rest of Africa. In addition, Ethiopia is Africa's oldest independent nation, and the only one to successfully resist colonization by Europeans, except for a five-year occupation by Italy from 1936 to 1941.

"Ethiopia has always held a special place in my own imagination and the prospect of visiting attracted me more strongly than a trip to France, England, and America combined. I felt I would be visiting my own genesis, unearthing the roots of what made me an African. Meeting the emperor himself would be like shaking hands with history."
—Nelson Mandela, 1961

LUCY OF LONG, LONG AGO

In 1974, American paleoanthropologist Donald Johanson discovered some fossilized bones in the Awash Valley of Ethiopia. Remarkably, Johanson's team found 40 percent of an ancient skeleton, including a jaw, an arm bone, a thigh bone, ribs, and vertebrae. The fossils turned out to be the bones of a female hominin who had lived some 3.2 million years ago. (A hominin is a primate belonging to the zoological family Hominini, which includes modern humans, extinct human species, and all immediate ancestral species.) During the excavation, the scientists played the Beatles' song "Lucy in the Sky with Diamonds" loudly on a tape recorder, and they named the specimen Lucy. She is now often called "the grandmother of humanity."

Lucy would become one of the most significant discoveries ever in the study of human evolution. She belonged to a new species called Australopithecus afarensis, *a previously undiscovered link between modern humans and our prehuman ancestors. When she lived, she was a full-grown adult who stood 3 feet 7 inches (1.1 m) tall and weighed 64 pounds (29 kilograms). Although her brain was small like a chimpanzee's, she walked upright like a modern human. Upright bipedal walking was a crucial development in the evolution of early humans which differentiated them from the ape species.*

For six years, from 2007 to 2013, an exhibition titled Lucy's Legacy: The Hidden Treasures of Ethiopia *toured the United States. It featured the actual Lucy fossil reconstruction and some one hundred artifacts from prehistoric times to the present. When Lucy returned to Ethiopia in May 2013, the country celebrated. Ethiopians call the Lucy skeleton "Dinkenesh," which means "you are wonderful."*

In 2015, US President Barack Obama "met" Lucy when he visited Ethiopia (the first sitting American president to ever visit the nation). "We honor Ethiopia as the birthplace of humankind," he said. "We are reminded that Ethiopians, Americans, all the people of the world are part of the same human family."

EARLY HUMAN ANCESTORS

Since the discovery of Lucy in 1974, researchers have found older and even more complete fossil remains of early human ancestors. In 2000, scientists in Ethiopia unearthed the remains of a 3.3 million year old *Australopithecus afarensis* baby they named Selam, meaning "peace" in the Amharic/ Ethiopian language. In 2001, the well-known Ethiopian paleoanthropologist Yohannes Haile-Selassie discovered 5.2 million-year-old bones related to the *Ardipithecus ramidus* family 15.5 miles (25 km) from Aramis. More recently, he has also found fossil specimens of other human ancestral species in the Afar region of Ethiopia. Such finds are of great significance in tracing human origins.

Archaeological evidence found in Ethiopia attests to the early hominid activity in the region. This evidence includes stone hand tools, sharp cutting instruments, and drawings found in limestone caves located near Dire Dawa. By approximately 5000 BCE, hunters and gatherers had established communities on the Ethiopian highlands. Grain cultivation and animal husbandry appeared in the northwest highlands some time before 2000 BCE.

Ancient cave paintings at Goda-Ajawa date back some five thousand years or more.

THE KINGDOM OF AXUM

Modern Ethiopia traces its origins to the great Kingdom of Axum (also spelled Aksum), one of Africa's most important cultural and trading centers during the first half of the first millennium CE. Migrants from southern Arabia laid the foundations of the kingdom by bringing their language and stone-building traditions to the northeastern African coast beginning around 1000 BCE. The Axumite kingdom began to take shape in the first century CE in the north and central portions of present-day Ethiopia. The kingdom became a thriving trading center in which merchants exchanged gold and ivory for cloth, glassware, tools, and other materials. Before the kingdom converted to Christianity, its people built huge burial pillars, or stelae, to mark the tombs of important leaders, according to pagan practice. The largest, the Great Stela (or Stele), rose 108 feet (33 m). Over time, most of these giant pillars fell to the ground and broke into pieces, probably due to structural collapse or earthquakes.

Christianity became the state religion of the Axumite kingdom during King Ezanas's rule in the fourth century. In an effort to stop pagan practices, he prohibited the building of any more stelae. In fact, the pillar called King Ezana's Stela, which stood 69 feet (21 m) tall, was probably the last one built. It remains standing today. The establishment of the Ethiopian Orthodox Church—heavily influenced by the Coptic Church in Egypt—would entrench the Christian tradition in Ethiopia for centuries to come. But other religious traditions also gained a foothold in Ethiopia. Judaism began spreading in the region in the early sixth century, and Islam started to gain converts along the coast two centuries later. The rise of Islam in the tenth and eleventh centuries led to the decline of Axum, as Christians retreated to the highlands and lost their preeminence in the kingdom's outlying regions.

THE ORIGINS OF THE ETHIOPIAN MONARCHY

Many of the legends surrounding the Ethiopian ruling dynasty originated in the fourteenth century. In this period, six scribes from the region of Tigray in north Ethiopia proclaimed that the country's monarchy was descended inability to effect further social and political reform, tried to overthrow his government while he was abroad. In 1962 Eritreans began their long armed struggle against Ethiopian rule and students clashed with police during demonstrations for Eritrean independence and for land and educational reform in the 1960s and 1970s. To make matters worse, a major famine broke out in the Tigray and Welo provinces between 1972 and 1974, causing the deaths of approximately two hundred thousand Ethiopians. By 1974, groups of students, workers, and soldiers were demanding the dismissal of Haile Selassie's cabinet. The emperor, then aged eighty-two, was unable to stem the rising tide of discontent. On September 12, 1974, a group of army officers deposed Haile Selassie and set up a new military government. The three-thousand-year-old Ethiopian monarchy had finally come to an end.

In August 1975, Haile Selassie died at the age of eighty-three while being held under house arrest by the new rulers. The official explanation was that he had died of complications related to a previous prostate operation. However, many Ethiopians believe to this day that he was assassinated by way of suffocation. The former emperor's remains were buried in an undisclosed place by the military government and for many years, the location was unknown. The bones were finally discovered in 1992 under a concrete slab on the grounds of his former palace. In November 2000, Haile Selassie was reburied by the Ethiopian Orthodox Church in Addis Ababa. Thousands of Ethiopians cried and applauded as their last emperor was laid to rest twenty-five years after his mysterious death.

THE STRUGGLE FOR ERITREA

Tension between Ethiopia and Eritrea began to intensify shortly after World War II. Following the war, the United Nations nullified Italian control over Eritrea and placed it under the Ethiopian crown as an autonomous territory. In 1962 Haile Selassie annexed Eritrea as a province of Ethiopia. Eritreans quickly established the Eritrean Liberation Front to spearhead their bid for independence. Few realized that thirty years of bitter struggle lay ahead.

After eight years of sporadic guerrilla warfare, a new Marxist group, the Eritrean People's Liberation Front (EPLF), gained control over the rebel forces

Colonel Mengistu Haile Mariam addresses a press conference in 1978.

The Mengistu government received significant economic and military assistance from the Soviet Union beginning in the late 1970s, and thus initially maintained a firm grip on power. But escalating crises at home began to cripple the regime by the 1980s. Insurgencies in Eritrea, Tigray, and Ogaden challenged the Ethiopian military machine more seriously than ever before. In 1983 a massive famine broke out in Ethiopia, claiming the lives of at least three hundred thousand people by 1985. Although a major international relief effort was launched to aid famine victims, these efforts were hindered by the government's policy of blocking food deliveries to regions it considered politically hostile.

By the mid- to late-1980s opposition to the Mengistu regime began to intensify, especially among leftist intellectuals, students, and workers. Representatives of various rebel groups soon united to form the Ethiopian People's Revolutionary Democratic Front (EPRDF). The EPRDF called for the removal of Mengistu and the establishment of a democratic government in Addis Ababa. It stepped up the armed struggle against Mengistu's forces in the late 1980s.

From 1989 to 1990 the breakup of the Soviet Union resulted in the collapse of Ethiopia's overseas support network; sources of much-needed economic aid could no longer be counted on. After rebel troops began closing in on Addis Ababa in May 1991, Mengistu fled to Zimbabwe and left his government to collapse. On May 28, 1991, the EPRDF took control of the capital and declared Meles Zenawi the country's interim president.

In 1994, Mengistu and seventy-two other members of his government were tried in an Ethiopian court for genocide, crimes against humanity, and the assassination of Haile Selassie. Megnistu and twenty-four others were tried in absentia. In 2006, after a twelve-year trial, Mengistu and all but one of the other officials were found guilty. The evidence against Mengistu included signed execution orders, videos of torture sessions, and personal testimonies. In 2011, the court sentenced Mengistu to death, again in absentia. However, it seems unlikely he will ever face justice as he remains in exile in Zimbabwe, which refuses to hand him over to Ethiopian authorities.

A NEW GOVERNMENT

Following the overthrow of the military rule in 1991, political and economic conditions began to stabilize. Once in power, Zenawi and his backers announced their support for a federal form of government in order to accommodate the needs of Ethiopia's many ethnic groups. The government organized local elections and accepted the independence oF Eritrea. In 1994, the Federal Democratic Republic of Ethiopia adopted a new constitution, leading to the nation's first multiparty elections. Most opposition parties chose to boycott these elections, ensuring a landslide victory for the EPRDF.

In 2000, Zenawi's government was reelected. In 2005, his ruling party again won a bitterly contested election, during which opposition demonstrations led to several deaths and many arrests. In 2012, Zenawi died and Hailemariam Desalegn became the country's new prime minister. (Hailemariam Desalegn is a patronymic name, in which Desalegn is the name of his father, Desalegn Boshe; therefore, according to custom, the man is referred to by his given name, or even as Mr. Hailemariam.) A close ally of Zenawi's, Hailemariam pledged to continue his "legacy without any change." From 2013 to 2014, he also served as the chairperson of the African Union.

INTERNET LINKS

www.bbc.com/earth/story/20141127-lucy-fossil-revealed-our-origins
BBC Earth presents the story of the discovery of Lucy, *Australopithecus afarensis*.

www.bbc.com/news/world-africa-13351397
BBC News presents a timeline of Ethiopia's history.

www.nytimes.com/learning/general/onthisday/bday/0723.html
This is the text of *The New York Times* obituary, "Haile Selassie of Ethiopia Dies at 83."

GOVERNMENT

Proud Ethiopians carry their nation's flag in Omo.

3

W E, THE NATIONS, NATIONALITIES, and peoples of Ethiopia:

Strongly committed, in full and free exercise of our right to self-determination, to building a political community founded on the rule of law and capable of ensuring a lasting peace, guaranteeing a democratic order, and advancing our economic and social development;

Firmly convinced that the fulfillment of this objective requires full respect of individual and people's fundamental freedoms and rights, to live together on the basis of equality and without any sexual, religious or cultural discrimination;

Further convinced that by continuing to live with our rich and proud cultural legacies in territories we have long inhabited, have, through continuous interaction on various levels and forms of life, built up common interest and have also contributed to the emergence of a common outlook ..."

So begins the Preamble to the Constitution of Ethiopia, which was ratified in 1994, and came into effect in 1995. This new constitution was written during a transitional period put in place after the overthrow of the Derg regime in 1991. Upon final ratification of the new constitution, Ethiopia's official name became the Federal Democratic Republic of Ethiopia (FDRE). The constitution provides autonomy to ethnically-based regions while reserving defense, foreign affairs, and constitutional issues for the federal government. This version of the constitution remains in effect today, and as such is the fundamental law of Ethiopia.

The Ethiopian flag has three equal horizontal bands of green, yellow, and red. In the center, a solid blue circle contains a yellow pentagram with yellow rays emanating from its angles. The green represents hope and the fertility of the land; yellow symbolizes justice and harmony; and red stands for sacrifice and heroism in the defense of the land. The blue symbolizes peace, and the pentagram represents the unity and equality of the peoples of Ethiopia.

GOVERNMENT STRUCTURE

The FDRE comprises the federal government, nine autonomous states with self-determining powers, and two administrative cities—Addis Ababa and Dire Dawa.

The federal government is headed by the prime minister, who is chosen by the parliament. The parliament is bicameral, or made of two houses—the 108-seat House of Federation and the 547-seat House of Peoples' Representatives. Together, these chambers comprise the legislative branch of the federal government. The House of Federation is responsible for interpreting the constitution and federal-regional issues, and the House of Peoples' Representatives is responsible for passing legislation. Representatives of both houses serve five-year terms. The House of Federation members are indirectly elected by state assemblies. The House of Peoples' representatives are elected by direct election, who in turn elect the president.

The House of Peoples' Representatives holds the highest authority of the federal government. The house is responsible to the Ethiopian people and has legislative power in all matters assigned to federal jurisdiction by the constitution. The political party or coalition of political parties with the greatest number of seats in the House of Peoples' Representatives forms

Although the judicial and legal systems are showing signs of independence, severe shortages of personnel and funding have hampered the effective operation of the courts. Law schools have been unable to produce enough competent lawyers. The courts in Ethiopia often step in to order the release of government critics jailed on trumped-up charges of treason or armed insurrection. However, judicial action often occurs only after unreasonably long delays, both because of the courts' enormous workload and because of excessive judicial deference to bad-faith police requests for additional time to produce evidence. In addition, courts have shown themselves far less likely to contest prolonged pretrial detention in high-profile cases that have the attention of high-level federal officials.

INTERNET LINKS

www.africa.upenn.edu/Hornet/Ethiopian_Constitution.html
A translation of the 1995 Ethiopian constitution can be found here.

www.cia.gov/library/publications/the-world-factbook/geos/et.html
The CIA World Factbook has up-to-date information about the Ethiopian government and its officials.

www.ethiopia.gov.et/government
This is the official site of the Ethiopian government portal, in English.

www.theguardian.com/global-development/2015/may/22/ethiopia-elections-controlled-political-participation
Written just before the 2015 elections, this article takes a look at the EPRDF and calls for the inclusion of dissenting voices in Ethiopian politics.

www.nytimes.com/2015/07/28/world/africa/obama-calls-ethiopian-government-democratically-elected.html
This article and video covers President Barack Obama's 2015 visit to Ethiopia, with the emphasis on how well its government is functioning.

ECONOMY

A tourist with a camera observes a male gelada baboon in Ethiopia's Simien Mountains.

4

AFRICA IS A CONTINENT OF SOME fifty-four countries and many of them are very poor. Ethiopia is one of the poorest; indeed, it is one of the most impoverished countries in the world. It ranks among the bottom fifteen nations on the 2015 UN Human Development Index—a composite measure of per capita income, health, and education. (In that index, all but one of the bottom twenty countries were in Africa.) About 37 percent of the Ethiopian population lived below the poverty line.

Nevertheless, the Ethiopian economy has shown solid growth in recent years, with a growth rate of 10.3 percent in 2014. The regime change in the 1990s brought about an economic change as well, with a transition from being centrally planned to being market oriented. Many previously state-owned properties have been privatized.

Agriculture remains the largest sector of the economy, but the government is pushing to diversify into manufacturing, textiles, and energy generation, and has attracted foreign investment in those sectors. In 2015, the government launched a second state-led Growth and Transformation Plan (GTPII), a five-year strategic framework for industrialization and urbanization, along with improved agricultural productivity. The first GTP ran from 2010 to 2015.

In 2015, the European Council on Tourism and Trade chose Ethiopia as the World's Best Tourism Destination for that year. Ethiopia beat out thirty other countries that were under consideration. The Ethiopian government hopes the honor will boost tourism revenues. It aims to attract more than 2.5 million foreign visitors by 2020, making tourism a major sector of the Ethiopian economy.

A boy plows the soil using a team of buffalo in Karat Konso, Ethiopia.

AGRICULTURE

Agriculture is by far the most important sector of the Ethiopian economy. In 2015 it constituted 41.4 percent of the country's GDP; about 85 percent of Ethiopians make a living by cultivating crops or raising livestock. The country's transportation and manufacturing sectors rely heavily on agricultural output as well.

Most of Ethiopia's arable land is farmed by peasant families who use only the most basic implements. An example would be the use of oxen for plowing. It is interesting to note that Ethiopia is the only place in Africa where oxen are used in this way. As noted by several economic historians, this is one of the similarities between Ethiopia's feudal system and Europe's. These rural dwellers tend to work on family plots and small-scale farms rather than on commercial farms.

Drought is a frequent occurrence, which points to the danger of having the economy rely so heavily on agriculture. As agricultural output remains variable and dependent on the climate, food shortages are a constant threat due to irregular rains and inadequate harvests. In addition, population growth

Coffea arabica, *or the coffee plant, still grows wild in the mountain forests of Ethiopia's southwest. In fact, Ethiopia is considered the birthplace of coffee. The word "coffee" itself might have come from the Kaffa region where the plant has been grown for centuries.*

Legend has it that some 1,200 years ago, a goatherd from Kaffa, in ancient Abyssinia (now Ethiopia), noticed his goats dancing and unable to sleep after eating some red berries. The herder then chewed some of the berries himself and felt a sense of heightened well-being. The mountain people took to chewing the berries for their stimulating effect, and eventually some people figured out how to roast, grind, and steep the beans to make a beverage. Traders eventually spread the Kaffa beans throughout the Middle East and Europe.

Coffee plays an important role in Ethiopian culture. It's also big business. With about 430,453 tons (390,500 metric tons) of coffee produced annually, it is the country's number-one export. In 2014, Ethiopia earned $780 million from coffee exports. The sector made up almost half of Ethiopia's gross domestic product, 84 percent of exports, and 80 percent of total employment. Ethiopia is the largest producer of coffee in Africa and the fifth largest producer in the world. Commonly exported Ethiopian coffees include the Sidamo, Yergacheffe, and Harer varieties.

In the town of Debark, a woman holds a handful of teff, one of Ethiopia's main subsistence crops.

has led to overcrowding, overgrazing, and soil erosion in many drought-prone areas, making farming a difficult and risky undertaking.

A number of crops are grown in Ethiopia, but none are as lucrative as the coffee bean. Coffee is the country's main cash crop and greatest foreign exchange earner. A high percentage of Ethiopian coffee is grown in the relatively well-watered southwestern portion of the country. Other products grown by Ethiopian farmers include grains such as teff (indigenous to Ethiopia), wheat, barley, corn, sorghum, and millet. The most common vegetables are chickpeas, lentils, haricot beans, cabbage, onions, and lettuce. Seeds, spices, tobacco, citrus fruit, and bananas are also cultivated.

Ethiopia is estimated to have the largest population of livestock on the African continent. The most common animals herded are sheep, goats, and cattle. Ethiopia is home not only to the largest cattle population in Africa but it is among the top ten cattle-producing countries in the world. Cattle have proven useful during Ethiopia's periodic droughts and furnish an array of goods for export. In fact, hides, skins, and leather goods are Ethiopia's second-largest exports after coffee.

MANUFACTURING

Manufacturing contributed about 15.6 percent of Ethiopia's GDP in 2015. Powered by hydroelectricity, most manufacturing plants are concentrated in Addis Ababa and Dire Dawa and produce consumer goods for the domestic market. Food and beverage processing and textiles dominate the country's manufacturing sector; other manufactured goods include leather goods, sugar and molasses, shoes, tobacco, and beeswax.

The Ethiopian manufacturing sector was plagued by a number of problems in the past, particularly shortages of foreign exchange, new investment, raw materials, and spare parts. The transitional government that took power in

1991 attempted to remedy some of these problems. It loosened investment regulations in an effort to attract foreign capital and offered new tax incentives to potential investors.

ENERGY

Wood, charcoal, and moving water are the primary sources of energy in Ethiopia. Reliance on wood and charcoal for energy and construction needs has contributed to the deforestation of much of the highlands during the last three decades. Hydropower meets about 88 percent of the country's electricity needs but this also means that electricity generation, like agriculture, is dependent on rainfall, which is unreliable in Ethiopia.

Natural gas reserves have been discovered and plans are afoot to exploit the estimated 440 trillion cubic feet (12.5 trillion cubic meters) of gas in the southeastern lowlands region. Officials hope to begin gas production and exports by 2017. China's GCL-Poly Petroleum Investments signed a production sharing deal with Ethiopia's mines ministry in late 2013 to develop the natural gas fields. Since Ethiopia has no access to the sea, the country also intends to construct a gas pipeline to its neighbor Djibouti, so the product can be shipped from its port on the Red Sea.

Exploration for oil is also under way in the Ogaden region. Unfortunately, the eight to ten million Somali ethnic population living in the area can sometimes be in the way. In 2013, the Ethiopian regime ordered its army in Ogaden to displace the rural population from large tracts of the Ogaden grassland by burning traditional pasture-rich areas in order to clear the land for oil exploration. This, in turn, only exacerbates local opposition and fuels an already-existing Somali rebel movement working for independence from Ethiopia.

TRANSPORTATION

Ethiopia's transportation system is somewhat dated, needing both upgrades and expansion. The country has about 27,563 miles (44,359 km) of roadways, of which fewer than 4,000 miles (6,437 km) are paved. Ethiopia's mountainous

The light rail service in Addis Ababa is a new addition to the city and its surrounding area.

terrain has made reaching remote areas notoriously difficult. Ethiopian officials, realizing that a modern transportation system is essential for economic growth, earmarked the equivalent of billions of dollars to build, upgrade, and repair roads under the Road Sector Development Program.

In 2015, the new Addis Ababa Light Rail system opened. Its two lines—one running north-south and one going east-west—have a combined length of almost 20 miles (31.6 km), and serve thirty-nine stations. It is the first light rail system to be built in sub-Saharan Africa, and can handle some fifteen thousand passengers per hour per direction. The railway was constructed by the China Railway Group and 85 percent financed by the Export-Import Bank of China.

Ethiopia is served by international airports at Addis Ababa, Dire Dawa, and several regional airports. Ethiopian Airlines (EAL) is the national airline, wholly owned by the government, and headquartered at Bole International Airport in Addis Ababa. It serves eighty-three international passenger destinations, and twenty domestic ones. Started in 1946, it is one of Africa's oldest airlines, and has been hailed as an African success story. In 2013, it had more than seven thousand employees, and, as of 2016, the airline had seventy-six aircraft in its fleet and another forty-six on order. In 2015, Ethiopian Airlines won the Best Regional Airline of the Year award at the Annual Airline Industry Achievement Awards by Air Transport World.

TOURISM

The EPRDF government has revived the Ethiopian tourist industry, after its dramatic slump during the Mengistu era. Besides making it easier for prospective tourists to qualify for visas and travel out of Addis Ababa, a number of new hotels are under construction in the capital and other popular tourist centers. In 2015, the Ethiopian Tourism Commission claimed that nearly 750,000 tourists came during fiscal year 2014—2015, generating $2.9 billion for the economy. Most of them came for the country's natural and historical attractions; others came to attend international conferences and meetings and to conduct business.

Ethiopia has no shortage of attractions for the adventurous tourist. Addis Ababa is rich with cultural diversity and has many places of interest. The countryside is home to fascinating ancient ruins such as the castles of Gonder, the rock-hewn churches of Lalibela, and the obelisks at Axum. Scenic wonders also abound. Not to be missed are the Blue Nile Gorge and the Blue Nile Falls near the town of Bahir Dar on Lake Tana. The Great Rift Valley lakes region is home to beaches, wildlife, and a popular hot springs resort. The Simien Mountains in the northwestern part of the country are renowned for their wildlife and scenic beauty. Many travelers discover why Ethiopia is known as "the Land of Thirteen Months of Sunshine."

INTERNET LINKS

www.cnn.com/2015/07/13/travel/ethiopia-worlds-best-tourism-destination
A photo gallery of Ethiopia's top tourist sites is found here.

equalexchange.coop/history-of-coffee-in-ethiopia
This page includes information about the economic role of coffee cooperatives in Ethiopia.

www.theafricareport.com/East-Horn-Africa/how-the-us-and-china-are-empowering-ethiopias-private-sector.html
This article discusses how both China and the United States are investing in Ethiopian manufacturing businesses.

ENVIRONMENT

The Blue Nile Falls in Bahir Dar are locally called *Tis Abay*, meaning "great smoke" in Amharic.

5

A LAND OF RUGGED MOUNTAINS, expansive savannas, lakes, and rivers, Ethiopia has long been recognized for its wealth of natural resources, endemic wildlife species, and biodiversity. The Great Rift Valley is a unique region of volcanic lakes, steep ridges, and spectacular vistas. The Blue Nile Falls is one of Africa's greatest natural wonders.

In 2015, Ethiopia joined the African Forest Landscape Restoration Initiative (AFR100), a new multinational program aimed at restoring 247 million acres (100 million hectares) of forest across the African continent by 2030.

This view of the Rift Valley shows its dramatic landscape.

With eighteen national parks and wildlife sanctuaries, Ethiopia has preserved a microcosm of the entire sub-Saharan ecosystem. Birdlife abounds and indigenous animals, from monkeys to the rare walia ibex, roam free. After the rains, the country is decked with flowers and is home to more native plants than most countries in Africa. Ethiopia's natural beauty has amazed visitors, but the country's environmental concerns are significant and are threatening the livelihood and well-being of its citizens, who are actually the key culprits of the environmental degradation.

ENVIRONMENTAL CONCERNS

The key environmental concern Ethiopia faces today is overpopulation, which results in overgrazing, overcultivation, soil erosion, deforestation, and desertification. Forest fires are also of critical concern.

More than 80 percent of Ethiopians, or about eighty million people, live in the country's rural highlands, where human and livestock population densities are very high and the overwhelming majority of Ethiopians earn their livelihoods from agricultural activities. The struggle to survive has resulted in a myriad of severe environmental concerns. Overgrazing and overcultivation have resulted in massive soil erosion, which affects 82 percent of the country. About 1 billion tons (907 billion kg) of topsoil is eroded annually, depleting the fertility of the land. There has also been a loss of vegetation cover and biodiversity due to deforestation and desertification. In 1900 approximately 30 percent of Ethiopia was covered by forest, but by the mid-1980s, this figure had fallen to less than 30 percent as forests were cleared to make room for agricultural cultivation. The gradual spread of the desert has shrunk the amount of land suitable for agriculture. From 1992 to 2002 there were 6,603 species of known plants, 277 species of mammals, and 262 bird species in the country. Since then 22 plant species along with 35 mammal and 22 bird species have become threatened.

Environmental degradation has had severe socioeconomic consequences for Ethiopians. With soil erosion, the depletion of soil fertility, desertification, and decreasing biodiversity, access to a variety of food and income sources has become increasingly difficult. Per capita food production has declined

WATER WOES

In 2004, Lake Haramaya vanished. The lake in Oromia, Ethiopia, had once been almost 10 miles (16 km) across and 25 feet (7.6 m) deep. It wasn't a huge lake, but fishermen earned their livelihoods from it, farmers used its water for irrigation, and the people in the surrounding region used it for their water supply. Now the lakebed is completely dry, and the water is unlikely to ever return. The reasons for the lake's demise point to the usual suspects: drought, lack of government oversight, population increase and excessive use, wasteful farming practices, and climate change.

Water is a huge problem for Ethiopia. Clean water is necessary to sustain life as well as for sanitation. In Ethiopia, access to clean drinking water and sanitation facilities is among the lowest in the world. A study conducted by Water.org found that only "42 percent of the population has access to a clean water supply" and only "11 percent of that number has access to adequate sanitation services." The CIA World Factbook, meanwhile, reports close to the same figures for 2015, with a somewhat better percentage—28 percent of the total population—for access to adequate sanitation facilities.

In this country, women and children walk to up to six hours to collect water, and often that water is from rivers or ponds shared by animals. In other words, the water is often contaminated. Waterborne illnesses, such as cholera or diarrhea, are the leading cause of death in children under five years old in Ethiopia—some thirty-three thousand children die every year from dirty water and poor sanitation. With inadequate water, people cannot bathe or even wash their hands often enough, which greatly increases the threat of disease. Extended droughts have created famines and led to conflicts with neighboring countries.

since the 1970s and food shortages are endemic in the Ethiopian highlands, where desertification is particularly severe and rainfall is marginal or unreliable. According to the United Nations and the World Bank, Ethiopia currently suffers from a food deficit so severe that even in the most productive year, at least five million Ethiopians require food aid. The United Nations and the World Bank maintain that without immediate steps to deal with the burgeoning population, large-scale environmental degradation, soil exhaustion, and rural landholding policies, Ethiopia will become permanently reliant upon donor support just to feed itself.

PROTECTED AREAS

Ethiopia is home to eighteen national parks and wildlife sanctuaries. These key biodiversity areas harbor the finest and most intact remnants of the highlands' original vegetation. They are also home to four threatened endemic species and to more than half of the global population of the Ethiopian wolf. What is even more remarkable is that more than thirty of the two hundred mammal species found in the Ethiopian highlands are found nowhere else, including three rodents and one primate—the gelada.

However, sharing these environmentally precious highlands are eighty million Ethiopians and their thousands of livestock. According to Conservation International, Ethiopia has the largest herd of domestic livestock and cattle in Africa. In protected areas like the Senkele Sanctuary, Netchsar National Park, Mago National Park, Awash National Park, and Simien Mountains National Park, thousands of cattle, goats, and sheep overrun the parks. These livestock increasingly must use areas with poor soil fertility to graze, and overgrazing has led to soil erosion and heightened competition between livestock and wildlife.

Complicating this mix are the intensive agricultural cultivation and human settlements in the area. Given the rapid conversion of natural habitats to areas of cultivation needed to feed the ever-increasing population, it is not surprising that almost all wildlife-sustaining habitats are being destroyed. In the Bale Mountains there are an estimated two hundred (of the global total estimate of four hundred) Ethiopian wolves, or Simien foxes. Outbreaks of

A herd of cattle in the Omo River Valley belongs to the Karo people.

rabies and canine distemper have killed up to 40 percent of the wolves in the Bale area in recent years, and continue to be a threat. It is thought that the diseases were carried by domestic dogs accompanying people and livestock in their seasonal search for grazing.

Hunting is also a significant problem in the Ethiopian highlands. Almost all the wildlife has been killed for food by tribal peoples, such as the Ari, Bana, Mursi, and Karo. Very few numbers of Beisa oryx, Grant's gazelle, and topi, formerly in the thousands, remain.

As the national parks are not adequately secured, staffed, or equipped, human causes of wildlife devastation cannot be stopped. These difficulties have been exacerbated by famines, refugee problems, civil unrest, armed rebellions, and war, which threaten the livelihood of people and make it unlikely that conservation measures will be enforced.

Currently, a few isolated pockets remain in Ethiopia where the depletion of vulnerable or endangered wildlife species is still considered reversible (including the Bale, Arusi, and Simien Mountains and the Denakil Desert). Outside recognized conservation areas, several remote locations of relatively low human population and activity, with quite high densities of wildlife, have been identified for sustainable use.

SIMIEN MOUNTAINS NATIONAL PARK *Home of the Ras Deshen Peak, the fourth-highest mountain in Africa, the Simien Mountain National Park is listed as a UNESCO World Heritage Site. It was added to the list in 1973, shortly after it was created in 1969. In 1996, the park was unfortunately added to the list of World Heritage in Danger, and it remains there to this day.*

The park was originally established primarily to protect the walia ibex that lived in the Simien Mountains. The walia ibex, or capra walie, is a goat found nowhere else in the world. By 1994–1996, the ibex population had fallen to about 200 to 250, mainly due to habitat loss and hunting. However, by 2004, the number had risen to about 500, but is still critically endangered.

Also found in the park are families of the unique gelada baboon, with its scarlet bleeding heart on its chest, and the rare Simien fox, or Ethiopian wolf. The Simien fox, although named after the mountains, is rarely seen here—in 2010, the population estimate here was 102—and is more likely to be seen in the Bale National Park. Over fifty species of birds have been sighted in the Simien Mountains.

AWASH NATIONAL PARK *Lying in the lowlands to the east of Addis Ababa, the Awash National Park is one of the finest reserves in Ethiopia. Awash National Park, surrounding the dormant volcano of Fantale, is a reserve of arid and semiarid woodland and savanna, with forests along the Awash River. Forty-six species of animals have been identified here, including beisa*

oryx and Swayne's hartebeest. The birdlife is prolific, especially along the river and on the nearby Lake Basaka, and there are endemic ones among the 392 species recorded.

OMO NATIONAL PARK *One of the most beautiful national parks in Ethiopia, the Omo National Park is home to an amazing range of wildlife. About 306 species of birds have been identified here, while large herds of eland, some buffalo, elephants, giraffes, cheetahs, lions, leopards, and Burchell's zebras are not uncommon.*

MAGO NATIONAL PARK *Covering an area of 1,343 miles (2,162 km) on the banks of the Omo River, the Mago National Park is relatively undeveloped for tourists. The broad grasslands teem with herds of buffalo, giraffes, elephants, and kudu, while sometimes it is possible to find lions, leopards, and Burchell's zebras. The abundant birdlife here is typical of dry grasslands and riverbanks.*

GAMBALA NATIONAL PARK *Many interesting species of animals and birds can often be seen here. According to the Wildlife Information Office, there are hundreds of species of birds—596 residents and 224 regular seasonal migrants residing in the park.*

BALE MOUNTAINS NATIONAL PARK
The Bale Mountains include Ethiopia's second-highest mountain but are not as rugged as the Simiens. The region is home to several of Ethiopia's endemic animals, including the Simien fox and mountain nyala. Like the walia ibex, the Simien fox, or Ethiopian wolf, is an endangered species. More than half of the existing population lives in the Bale Mountains, numbering around 210 animals. Some of the wolves in the region have hybridized with domestic dogs.

The Simien wolf

The Nile River, Africa's longest river, is most often associated with Egypt. However, its water resources are shared by eleven countries, including Ethiopia. The river's two main tributaries are the White Nile and the Blue Nile, which flow together in Sudan to form the Nile itself. The Blue Nile rises from Lake Tana in the Ethiopian Highlands. The Blue Nile provides most of the water to the main Nile. Egyptians rely heavily on the waters of the Nile and were therefore concerned when Ethiopia began to build a huge dam on the Blue Nile.

Construction of the Grand Ethiopian Renaissance Dam began in 2011, with a 2017 opening date. When completed, it will be the largest hydroelectric dam in Africa and the eleventh largest in the world. During the construction, Egypt launched vigorous objections. Egypt fears the dam will cause a permanent reduction in the waters of the Nile. Although Ethiopia reputes that claim, the eventual impact on the downstream water volume is essentially unknown. The project caused political conflict between the nations, as Egypt claimed the construction of the dam violates a 1959 treaty that gives Sudan and Egypt exclusive rights to the Nile's waters.

CONSERVATION EFFORTS

While Ethiopia is blessed with abundant natural assets, they remained largely unprotected until the mid-1960s, when the government instituted an environmental conservation program. Since then, Ethiopia has enacted a wide range of laws aimed at protecting the environment. The incorporation of environmental rights under the constitution, the adoption of the Environmental Policy and the Conservation Strategy of Ethiopia, the ratification of multilateral environmental conventions, and the establishment of the Environmental Protection Authority are some of the basic steps taken toward environmental protection and sustainable development.

The results, however, have not been spectacular. The conservation efforts have not been able to stop people from threatening the wildlife and vegetation within the protected areas. The inadequacy of Ethiopia's conservation efforts can be attributed to several factors, including ineffective deterrents, such as fines that are modest compared with the gains that would be gotten from noncompliance, and the lack of specific regulations and laws, standards, and guidelines that could be implemented and monitored.

INTERNET LINKS

www.theguardian.com/sustainable-business/2016/may/02/ethiopia-famine-drought-land-restoration
This article focuses on the connection between drought and soil erosion in Ethiopia.

www.internationalrivers.org/campaigns/grand-ethiopian-renaissance-dam
This site offers an article and fact sheet about the Grand Ethiopian Renaissance Dam.

www.iucnredlist.org/details/3797/0
The walia ibex entry on the IUCN Red List of Threatened Species is detailed here.

www.pbs.org/frontlineworld/stories/africa705/history/africa.html
This site includes a slideshow and an audio report about the disappearance of Lake Haramaya.

whc.unesco.org/en/list/9
This is the UNESCO World Heritage entry for Simien National Park, which includes a photo gallery.

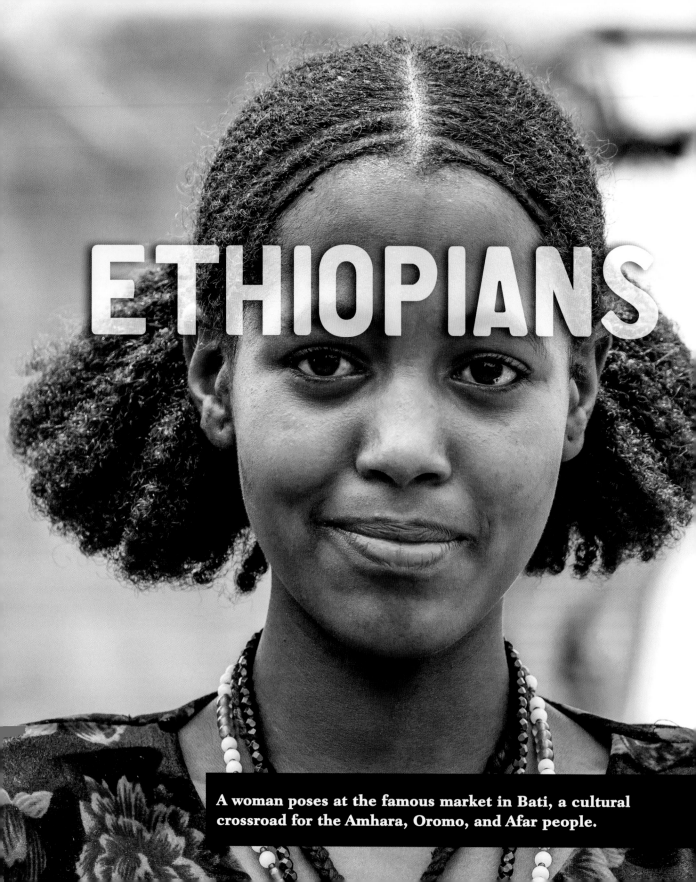

ETHIOPIANS

A woman poses at the famous market in Bati, a cultural crossroad for the Amhara, Oromo, and Afar people.

6

O NE OF THE MOST REMARKABLE aspects of Ethiopia is its cultural diversity. The country is home to more than one hundred different ethnic groups, the largest of which are the Oromo, Amhara, Tigray, and Somali. More than seventy languages are spoken in the country. Ethiopia's diversity has greatly enriched the country over the centuries, but it has also led to conflict.

The Amhara group played a dominant role through much of Ethiopia's history, but resistance to Amhara power became widespread in the late 1970s. Undeterred by Mengistu's military might, ethnic secessionist movements led by Eritreans, Oromos, Tigrayans, and Somalis severely threatened Ethiopian unity. By 1991, the Eritreans had won their independence, and the EPRDF—made up mostly of Tigrayans—toppled the Mengistu government.

POPULATION STATISTICS

In 2015 approximately 99.5 million people lived in Ethiopia, 80 percent of whom lived in rural areas, cultivating crops or herding livestock. The country's birthrate in 2015 was 37.27 births per 1,000 people, about on par with other developing nations in sub-Saharan Africa, but much higher than the world average of 18.6 per 1,000. Its death rate of

An Oromo girl sells her wares at the market in Harer.

8.19 deaths per 1,000 people is down considerably from the rate ten years before, at 14.86 per 1,000. Ethiopia's infant mortality rate, which is defined as the number of infants per 1,000 live births who die before their first birthday, was approximately 53 per 1,000 in 2015. This is down from 94 per 1,000 live births ten years before. The reasons for the high infant mortality rate include Ethiopia's lack of health-care facilities, the spread of infectious diseases, poor sanitation, malnutrition, and food shortages. These factors, combined with the AIDS epidemic, which continues to impact Ethiopia, make the life expectancy of Ethiopians one of the lowest in the world. Current figures estimate that an Ethiopian girl born in 2015 can expect to live to age sixty-four, and a boy can expect to live to age fifty-nine. The Ethiopian life expectancy averages, like others mentioned here, have improved over the past ten years.

ETHNIC GROUPS

The Oromo people constitute 34.4 percent of Ethiopia's population and are the country's largest ethnic group. Ancestors of contemporary Oromo society started to spread out from their original homeland in the south central highlands in the sixteenth century. Today their descendants live in central, southern, and western Ethiopia. Although the members of this ethnic group come from a line of pastoralists and nomads and share the Oromo language, there is much diversity within the group. For example, some Oromo live in decentralized groups, while others live in communities characterized by hierarchical authority structures. Religious beliefs among the Oromo can vary as well. Some Oromo hold traditional beliefs, while other family members may practice Islam or Orthodox Christianity.

The Amhara and Tigray combined make up 33 percent of Ethiopia's population. The dominant group during centuries of imperial rule, the Amhara have continued to play a leading role in Ethiopian politics, despite their minority status. The Amhara language, Amharic, has long been the favored medium of communication in government, commerce, and education, and is the official language of Ethiopia. Most of the Amhara belong to the Ethiopian Orthodox Church and tend farms in the Ethiopian highlands, where they cultivate teff, barley, wheat, sorghum, corn, and peas, and herd cattle, sheep, and goats. Occasional conflicts among the Amhara of different regions attest to the group's lack of cohesiveness.

Like the Amhara, the Tigray also farm in the highlands and tend to belong to the Ethiopian Orthodox Church. The Tigray are known for having founded the kingdom of Axum in the early centuries of the Christian era. Their descendants have lived in the area around Axum for centuries, and because of this, the soil in the region has become largely exhausted. The resulting poor harvests have led many Tigray to move to other areas of the country in search of better land. The Tigray speak Tigrinya, a Semitic language related to Amharic.

The fourth key ethnic group is the Somali, making up about 6.2 percent of Ethiopians. Predominantly pastoralists, the Somalis are concentrated in the Ogaden, the region in the southeastern lowlands near the border with Somalia. Many Somalis are Muslims whose ancestors converted to Islam around the twelfth century.

OTHER GROUPS IN ETHIOPIA

SIDAMA The Sidama constitute 4 percent of the total Ethiopian population. These people occupy a densely populated area in southwestern Ethiopia that is reputed for its fertile soil. An agricultural people, they grow grain crops, coffee, tobacco, and a banana-like crop known as *enset*. They also raise cattle, sheep, and horses. Like other Ethiopians, religious observance among the Sidama can involve traditional beliefs, Christianity, or Islam.

SHANKELLA The Shankella, an ethnic group that constitutes approximately 4 percent of the population, occupies the western part of the country from the border of Eritrea to Lake Turkana.

STYLES OF DRESS AND ADORNMENT

One of the most distinctive articles of clothing for rural Ethiopians is the shamma *(SHEH-mah), a one-piece cotton wrap worn over the shoulders and arms. Worn by both men and women, the shamma is particularly common among the Amhara and Tigray peoples. This garment often features a colorful border and is sometimes worn for ceremonial occasions by city dwellers as well as country people. In the higher mountainous regions the shamma is useful in keeping out the cold wind.*

Another traditional costume is the k'amis *(kah-MEES), a white cotton gown that women sometimes wear beneath the shamma. Western-style dress is now a common sight in urban areas, although people may wear more traditional clothing at home.*

Earrings, bracelets, necklaces, and religious emblems are popular forms of adornment in Ethiopia and are often made of beads or shells. Oromo women are known for their attractive necklaces, while Tigray women are famous for their gold jewelry. Scarves and turbans are worn by women throughout the country. Men in the rural areas often carry walking sticks—known in Ethiopia as dulas *(DOO-luhs)—as they roam the countryside.*

GURAGE The Gurage, about 2.5 percent of the population, reside in the southern Shewa region, just north of their Sidama neighbors. They are also agriculturalists whose religious beliefs can vary. However, unlike the Sidama, the Gurage have established a notable presence in Ethiopia's urban areas, where they engage in trade, manual labor, and other service occupations.

AFAR Sometimes referred to as the Danakil, the Afar people live in the rocky, arid countryside between the highlands and the Red Sea. The Afar people are mainly pastoralists.

PEOPLE ON THE WESTERN BORDER These groups include the Nara, Kunama, Gumuz, Berta, Anuak, and Nuer. They occupy remote lowland areas near Sudan and speak Nilo-Saharan languages, unlike the rest of Ethiopians (the majority of Ethiopians speak Afro-Asiatic languages). Many of these borderland peoples are descendants of slaves held by Ethiopian and Sudanese Arabs in the nineteenth and early twentieth centuries. Today these groups engage in cultivation, herding, and fishing. Their remote location has long kept them on the periphery of Ethiopian society.

SOCIAL STRATIFICATION

During the era of imperial rule, social status in Ethiopia depended on the amount of land one owned. But once the old order was overthrown and Mengistu came to power, land was nationalized, so social status became more closely tied to one's political influence. Party members, government ministers, military officers, and senior civil servants became the new elite from the mid-1970s onward.

Today Ethiopians tend to view government work, military service, religious leadership, and farming as the most desirable occupations. Forming the middle class in Ethiopia are those in the bureaucracy and the professionals, many of whom have advanced educational training. Middle-class Ethiopians are highly urbanized and frequently marry across ethnic boundaries. Many left the country during the Mengistu era. People engaged in commerce and trade—many of whom are Muslims or non-Ethiopians—have yet to enjoy the respect that is bestowed upon bureaucrats and professionals.

INTERNET LINKS

www.cia.gov/library/publications/the-world-factbook/geos/et.html
The CIA World Factbook has up-to-date statistics and information about the Ethiopian population.

www.famousbirthdays.com/birthplace/ethiopia.html
This site lists some of Ethiopia's most famous people, including some from history and many of today's celebrities.

www.thelovelyplanet.net/traditional-dress-of-ethiopia-colors-of-ethiopian-culture
This site shows the various kinds of traditional costumes in Ethiopia.

LIFESTYLE

A family belonging to the Dassanech tribe stands outside their home in the Omo Rift Valley.

JUST AS THERE IS NO SINGLE Ethiopian culture, there is no single Ethiopian lifestyle. The country's cultural diversity has created many different lifestyles that vary according to religion, ethnicity, gender, generation, and locale—such as rural versus urban, and highlands versus lowlands.

As in most countries, the family is the basic social and economic unit of the nation, regardless of region or ethnic group. Ethiopian families tend to be larger than North American families—the average size of an Ethiopian household is 4.8 people compared with North America's 2.6 people. This is partly because parents fear that some of their offspring will die from famine or disease. Sometimes families are nuclear, consisting only of parents and their children. Other Ethiopian families are extended, meaning that an assortment of aunts, uncles, cousins, and grandparents share the household.

Families in Ethiopia tend to be patriarchal, but women are crucial in holding families together. The division of labor between men and women is usually well defined, especially in rural areas. Men are expected to plant, weed, and harvest the family's crops; women, besides helping with the farm work, also cook and prepare food, maintain the home, and assume primary responsibility for child care. Elders are treated with great respect.

Ethiopia lies in the East Africa Time (EAT) zone, but many Ethiopians have their own way of telling time, which is baffling to the rest of the world. They use a twelve-hour clock with one cycle of 1 to 12 from dawn to dusk and another from dusk to dawn. Daytime begins at dawn; therefore 7 a.m. EAT is 1:00 Ethiopian time, and 12:00 noon EAT time is 6:00 Ethiopian time.

BIRTH AND CHILDHOOD

A boy carries his little brother on his back in Axum.

Like many developing countries, Ethiopia has a high infant mortality rate, and this explains why births are sometimes greeted cautiously by parents, especially fathers. Only a minority of Ethiopian children are born in hospitals. Most are born in rural households, where elderly women often serve as midwives to assist expectant mothers. In families belonging to the Ethiopian Orthodox Tewahedo Church, boys are baptized on the fortieth day after birth and girls on the eightieth. Sometimes children are given a special baptismal name that remains a secret or is used only by the immediate family. Friends and relatives are usually invited to baptism ceremonies, and they help mark the occasion by serving food and drink.

Ethiopian children are given responsibilities at an early age. When they reach about five years of age, rural children may be asked to help gather firewood or feed their family's chickens. When they are a little older, children often help guard their family's fields from intruders such as birds or baboons. Boys are eventually expected to help herd goats and cattle, while girls generally help grind grain, prepare meals, and care for younger children.

Childhood in rural Ethiopia is not all work, however. Children have ample time for play and often participate in games and recreational activities with their peers. Young people also participate fully in religious festivals, during which they can enjoy feasts, dances, music, and fellowship.

MARRIAGE

Although marital practices in Ethiopia vary according to ethnic group, some generalizations can be made. Women often marry while still in their teens, while men tend to marry in their late teens or early twenties. Marriages can

NAMING CONVENTIONS IN ETHIOPIA

Ethiopians do not use family names (the surname used as a last name in most Western cultures). Usually an Ethiopian person has an individual name followed by one or more patronymics. This is typically his or her father's first name, which may then be followed by the grandfather's first name. People in the West sometimes confuse this patronymic name as a surname, but it is not because the name changes with each new generation. Likewise, when an Ethiopian woman marries, she does not change her name to her husband's patronymic, because it is not a family name.

When using a title of respect, therefore, to address a man named Abebe Emanuel, for example, it would be incorrect to call him Mr. Emanuel, but rather he should be addressed Mr. Abebe. Ethiopians use the titles of Ato (Mr.), Weizaro (Mrs.), and Weizerit (Miss) followed by the person's first name.

occur across religious lines—between Christians and Muslims, for example— but in these cases, either the bride or the groom usually converts. Marriages rarely cross both religious and ethnic lines.

Negotiations between the bride's family and the groom's family typically take place prior to the wedding and involve both male and female elders. The groom's family is usually expected to offer a gift to the bride's family, to compensate them for their loss. This gift, known as bridewealth, is given in many traditional African societies to sanction marriage. In most cases, if a marriage ends in divorce, the bridewealth is returned to the groom's family.

Ethiopian weddings tend to involve an elaborate array of rituals. Some groups hold solemn engagement ceremonies prior to weddings. In one such ceremony, the groom's mother anoints her son and his best man on the forehead and knee, then leads a procession to the bride's family home. There, the groom and the best man are anointed by the bride's mother. In some Muslim wedding ceremonies, the groom and the best man have black markings drawn around their eyes and crosses painted on their foreheads. They then join a wedding procession led by elders carrying fly whisks and wearing fine clothes. Ethiopian wedding ceremonies are usually presided over by a religious official who witnesses the exchange of vows.

In Lalibela, a man places a wedding ring on his bride's finger during the solemn ceremony.

After the ceremony, it is time for feasting. Dances and chanting competitions are sometimes held as well. In many wedding receptions, the groomsmen will share the same table, while the bride and groom exchange mouthfuls of food in front of the assembled guests. Following the celebrations, many newlyweds go on a honeymoon in which they stay in a special hut and enjoy attentive service from the groomsmen for a week or two.

DEATH

The customs surrounding death in Ethiopia also differ according to religion, ethnicity, and region. In most highland societies, funerals can take several days and draw even more people than weddings. Two terms are commonly used in the highlands to refer to funeral ceremonies: *merdo* (MUHR-doh), which means announcement of death, and *legso* (LEHK-soh), which refers to mourning. Christian communities often have restrictions governing proper burials. For example, such communities may refuse to give a Christian burial to a suicide victim or a person who married a Muslim. They also often oppose burying Christians in the same cemeteries with Muslims.

Burial associations are common among Ethiopians. Besides providing members with a sense of community, these associations ensure that their members will be given a proper burial. Members are expected to attend the funerals of association members and to make regular contributions to the association. Typical contributions include wood, water, grain, money, and prepared food items. Most burial associations have a leader or leaders who collect donations and enforce rules. In rural Wello society, such associations are known as the *qire* (KEE-ray); in some Amhara areas, the term used is *iddir* (ID-ir).

RURAL LIVING

Approximately 90 percent of Ethiopians make their living from the land. After the imperial government was toppled in 1974, private land ownership was abolished. The nobles and landowners who had controlled so much of the land were forced to surrender their privileges to the new regime. The land redistribution program mandated by the Mengistu-led government involved forcing thousands of peasants onto collective farms. Private property rights were reinstated by the new transitional government in the early 1990s, and the mandatory collective farming programs have been discontinued.

Housing styles in the Ethiopian countryside vary by region and ethnic group. Cooking is done in a fireplace in the middle of the house. Sometimes, families reserve a corner of their home for a few of their domesticated animals. Although villages can be found throughout Ethiopia, more common are smaller clusters of two to four homes surrounded by fields and gardens.

Nomadic Ethiopians—most of whom live in the arid lowland regions—often live in portable homes constructed of branches, grass, and animal skins. These homes are easily disassembled and transported on the backs of camels as the nomads travel the plains looking for new grasslands and sources of water. Northern rural dwellers sometimes live in houses made of stone.

URBAN LIVING

Housing in Ethiopia's cities reflects patterns of social inequality and thus varies a great deal. Some high government officials and prosperous business people live in spacious homes with appliances, telephones, and several cars. Members of the urban underclass, on the other hand, are sometimes forced by economic circumstance to live in small tin shacks without running water or electricity. Urban poverty is a serious problem in Addis Ababa, giving rise to overcrowding, homelessness, and an increasing number of street children. Inadequate municipal governance in providing sanitary living conditions and access to clean water and electricity exacerbates urban poverty and makes the cities hotbeds for crime and diseases.

Urbanization has altered traditional family structures and social roles in Ethiopia. Whereas rural women tend to be confined to household tasks, women in urban areas have more opportunities to work outside the home, for example, in schools, businesses, hotels, and restaurants. The urban environment has also affected young people's lives. As the demand for housing and well-paying jobs in Addis Ababa often exceeds the supply, many young adults have felt obligated to postpone marriage until they achieve economic security and independence. This often takes longer in the city than it does in the countryside.

A poor neighborhood in Harer has small shacks and old cars.

ETHIOPIAN WOMEN

Women have traditionally been relegated to a subordinate status in Ethiopian society. They have faced persistent discrimination and have had fewer opportunities for education and employment outside of the home. However, as Ethiopia has changed, so too has the role of its women.

In the rural areas women are expected to be wives and mothers first and foremost. Women's tasks typically include raising children, maintaining the household, grinding corn, carrying loads, washing clothing, and helping with the farm work. Hard physical labor is something that most rural women are used to. Cooking in particular takes up a large chunk of their time.

Women's roles began to change somewhat in the 1970s and 1980s, as Ethiopia's wars took many men away from their homesteads. Women were left to do the bulk of the farming, support the family, and care for the children and older relatives on their own. Many women therefore became the heads of their households and emerged from this era with new responsibilities and a heightened sense of independence.

Urban Ethiopian women usually have more opportunities for education, health care, and employment than their rural counterparts. Women in cities and towns have typically worked in the service sector, in establishments such as hotels and restaurants. Other employment opportunities for urban women include factory work and sales.

Even though the constitution states that all persons are equal before the law and that there shall be no discrimination based on gender, age, religion, and so forth, there have been no effective enforcements of this law. But despite a long history of discrimination, many women regard cities as places where economic independence can be achieved. Some flee the rural areas in order to escape arranged or unhappy marriages; they quickly find work in Addis Ababa as waitresses or domestic servants. Some women even travel as far as the Middle East to seek employment as industrial or domestic workers.

SCHOOLS AND STUDENTS

Improving educational opportunities for a large and dispersed population has been one of modern Ethiopia's major challenges. In 1974 the literacy rate in Ethiopia was less than 10 percent. The Mengistu regime undertook a massive literacy campaign beginning in the late 1970s and claimed that the country's literacy rate had increased to 63 percent by 1984. Although this was probably an inflated figure, strides were undoubtedly made. In 2015, the literacy rate

Children of different ages crowd together at a school in the town of Jinka in southern Ethiopia.

among Ethiopians was about 49 percent, with 57 percent of men being able to read and write, compared to only 41 percent of women.

Education is free from primary through university level. (However, many families still cannot afford the additional costs of clothing, books and supplies, and transportation.) Primary education from grades one to six begins at seven years of age. Secondary education from grades seven to twelve begins at thirteen years of age. Education is compulsory at the primary level and primary schools are scattered across the countryside.

Thereafter, access to facilities determines further education, which may explain why children attending secondary schools are more prevalent in larger urban areas. Consequently, enrollments decline drastically from the primary to the secondary level, and many secondary school facilities are severely overtaxed.

In 2012, 95.5 percent of children in the relevant age groups were enrolled in primary schools. That appears to be an excellent statistic, but drop-out rates are very high. Only about half of the children who begin in grade one go on to complete primary school. The enrollment and attendance rates for secondary school are much lower. Less than 10 percent of children graduate from high school.

Urban schools tend to be more numerous and better equipped than rural ones, which are often relatively inaccessible due to the country's underdeveloped transportation network. Rural schools have long suffered from poor facilities and shortages of teaching staff. Since many rural families are traditionally reluctant to send their daughters to school, students in the countryside are predominantly male. Girls growing up in the cities, however, are more likely to attend school than their rural counterparts, and they can now attend a university if they score well enough in national examinations.

Ethiopia has approximately a dozen universities and colleges providing technical, teaching, and other professional training, but the country's most prestigious institution of higher learning is Addis Ababa University. Established in 1950 as Haile Selassie I University, the institution was renamed by the socialist government in the mid-1970s. As it stands now, higher education is still beyond the reach of most Ethiopians. The exceptions are in Addis Ababa. In recent years, a number of private schools have sprung up to meet the demand for university-level instruction in the capital city, as space limitations at Addis Ababa University make for an extremely competitive admissions process at the premier institution.

The educational system in Ethiopia clearly faces many challenges. Due to rural economic conditions, many families have trouble finding money for their children's school supplies. They also find it difficult to send their children to school when they are needed to herd livestock, work in the fields, and help with domestic chores. These socioeconomic realities have made finishing high school difficult for most rural youths. Wartime damage to schools and shortages of teachers, books, and desks only add to these problems. But with the right combination of internal political stability, economic development, and international assistance, education in Ethiopia will continue to improve.

ETHIOPIANS ABROAD

Between 1974 and 1991 approximately 3.5 million Ethiopians left their country in search of a better life. Another twenty thousand people fled immediately after the fall of the Mengistu regime in mid-1991. Many of those who fled during the Mengistu era did so to escape violence and political persecution; others left because of religious or ethnic discrimination. Some emigrants left in search of better economic opportunities.

Neighboring countries in East Africa and the Horn absorbed many of the Ethiopians. In the mid-1980s thousands of Ethiopians fled into Sudan, Djibouti, and Somalia to escape warfare. By 1988 over half a million Ethiopian refugees were living in Sudan alone. This mass exodus of Ethiopians resulted in a serious humanitarian crisis, as the refugees' need for food, shelter, and medical supplies far outstripped Sudan's ability to provide.

Many Ethiopians settled in the United States during this same period. Although some sought US citizenship, many still actively monitored the political situation back home, sometimes staging meetings and marches or publishing newsletters relating to current events in Ethiopia. The struggle for Ethiopians living in the United States has been to adjust to a new culture without losing touch with their Ethiopian heritage. Sizable communities of Ethiopian expatriates now exist in metropolitan areas such as Washington, DC, and the San Francisco Bay Area.

LIVING WITH AIDS

The AIDS, acquired immune deficiency syndrome, epidemic hit Ethiopia hard. At the end of 2003, the UN reported that about 1.5 million Ethiopian adults had AIDS or human immunodeficiency virus (HIV), the forerunner of AIDS.

HIV is generally spread through sexual contact, intravenous drug use, or perinatal transmission, which means the disease is spread from mother to newborn. Many of the infected, for fear of being ostracized, refrain from revealing their health status, thus enabling the infection to spread further. In addition, poverty often makes medical treatment inaccessible. Having a significant number of the population affected by AIDS is economically draining. The vicious cycle of poverty is made even more pronounced because those stricken with AIDS are often unable to work.

According to Ethiopia's HIV/AIDS Prevention and Control Office, more than 70,000 people died of AIDS in 2010. By 2015, the death rate had fallen by 70 percent. However, some 730,000 people were still living with HIV. Ethiopia has been working to address the crisis in the following areas: intensifying HIV prevention; enhancing care, treatment, and support; and generating and using vital information. Prevention activities have included programs in schools, universities, and youth centers to encourage young people to change their sexual behavior. Measures like condom distribution and establishing Voluntary Counseling and Testing (VCT) Centers—where people voluntarily test themselves for HIV and disclose their health status—as well as enforcing stricter controls for screening potential blood donors have met with slow but growing success.

Meanwhile, Ethiopia's children suffer the effects of the AIDS epidemic. In 2014, some 110,000 children under the age of fifteen had the illness themselves, and some 450,000 children under eighteen had been orphaned due to AIDS.

INTERNET LINKS

www.numbeo.com/cost-of-living/country_result.jsp?country=Ethiopia
This site lists the prices of various goods in Ethiopia, for purposes of comparing the cost of living.

olsonfarlow.com/portfolios/ethiopias-omo-valley-march-2010-national-geographic-magazine
This extraordinary photo gallery examines the lives of the tribal people who live in Ethiopia's Omo River Valley.

www.unaids.org/en/regionscountries/countries/ethiopia
This site has up-to-date statistics on AIDS in Ethiopia.

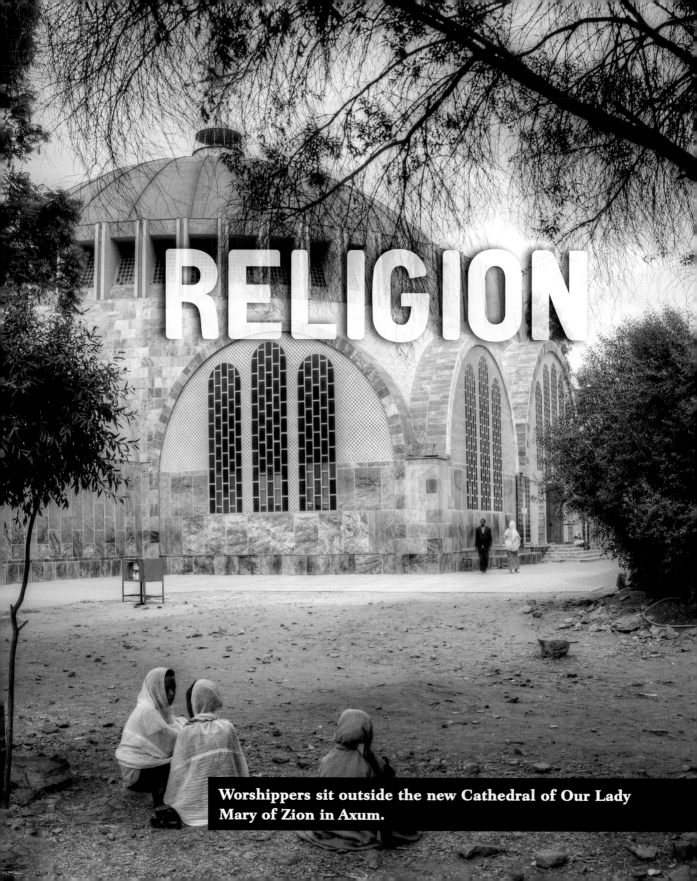

RELIGION

Worshippers sit outside the new Cathedral of Our Lady Mary of Zion in Axum.

8

E THIOPIA'S DIVERSE RELIGIOUS tapestry has created a great legacy of art and architecture. Religious groups and organizations also play a vital role in Ethiopia's festivals, music, education, and cultural life.

The country is home to both Christianity and Islam. In the southern regions, Muslim majorities predominate, representing about 34 percent of the country's population. Christians, belonging mostly to the Ethiopian Orthodox Church, constitute about 63 percent of Ethiopians.

The Chapel of the Tablet in Axum houses the purported Ark of the Covenant.

The most important Ethiopian Orthodox church, Our Lady Mary of Zion in Axum, claims to house the original Ark of the Covenant, the chest containing the two stone tablets of the Ten Commandments that God gave to Moses. According to tradition, Menelik I brought the Ark to Ethiopia after he visited his father King Solomon, ruler of the ancient Kingdom of Israel.

Ethiopian Orthodox followers sing and chant during a procession as part of the Timkat celebration of Epiphany.

Closely related to the Coptic Church of Egypt, the Ethiopian Orthodox Church was founded in the fourth century, long before the arrival of European missionaries. Tewahedo is a Ge'ez word meaning "being made one" and reflects the church's understanding of Christ as having one nature.

CHRISTIANITY

The overwhelming majority of Ethiopia's Christians belong to the Ethiopian Orthodox Tewahedo Church, which has the allegiance of approximately 43.5 percent of the country's people, among whom the Amhara and Tigray ethnic groups are particularly well represented.

The roots of the Ethiopian Orthodox Church stretch back to ancient times. It was established in the fourth century CE, when Christianity became the state religion of the Axumite kingdom. This occurred around the same time that Emperor Constantine made Christianity the official religion in Rome in 325 CE. The church's influence soon became intertwined with that of the Ethiopian monarchy; so much so that it remained the official state church in Ethiopia through the era of Haile Selassie. As the church's traditions came directly from the Middle East, its version of Christianity differed from that spread by European missionaries in Africa later on. Drawing heavily on Old Testament traditions and scriptures, the Ethiopian Orthodox Tewahedo Church developed separately from Western Christianity.

The church's great power and influence in Ethiopian society remained intact for centuries. However, by the 1950s some educated Amharas and Tigrayans began to question the church's political and economic domination and its many privileges. After Haile Selassie was forced from power, the Mengistu regime seized the landholdings of the church, divesting much of its power and imprisoning many of the religious leaders. While these measures altered the organization of the church, they did little to weaken the beliefs of its followers.

Members of the Ethiopian Orthodox Tewahedo Church believe in God and an array of angels and saints. Some church adherents blend Christian beliefs with traditional African beliefs, as is common in much of the continent. To demonstrate their faith, the laity are required to fast more than two hundred days annually, including every Wednesday and Friday, and during Lent and Easter.

In contrast to most Christian churches in the West, Ethiopian Orthodox Churches are usually circular or octagonal in shape. Their interiors tend to be divided into three main parts. The outer ring is where most parishioners stay during church services; it also provides space for clergy to sing hymns and perform dances. Worshippers are usually expected to remove their shoes before entering an Ethiopian Orthodox Church. In some churches, women are not allowed to enter. The middle ring is designed for communion and is limited to those who have fully honored church precepts, such as the observance of fasts during designated days. The inner sanctum houses a sacred ark dedicated to the church's patron saint. This ark is retrieved by priests during religious ceremonies and is occasionally taken outside for church processions. Only priests may enter the inner sanctum of an Ethiopian Orthodox Church.

Ethiopia is also home to about five hundred thousand Catholics, of whom approximately one-third adhere to the Ethiopian rite and two-thirds to the

Latin rite. Ethiopia's Protestant denominations include the Fellowship of Evangelical Believers, Lutheran, Presbyterian, and Seventh-Day Adventist churches. The country also hosts branches of the Armenian Orthodox Church and the Greek Orthodox Church.

ISLAM

Practiced in Ethiopia for more than one thousand years, Islam is an all-encompassing religion that permeates the daily life of those who practice it. More than a religion, Islam is a culture and a way of life. It was first developed in Arabia in the seventh century, when the Prophet Muhammad claimed to have received the word of God—God being known as Allah in Islam—through a series of divine revelations. These revelations were later recorded in the Qur'an, the Muslim holy book. Muslims around the world over are required to practice Islam's five pillars of faith: (1) recitation of the *shahada*, proclaiming faith in Allah and Muhammad; (2) prayer five times daily; (3) almsgiving;

Muslims perform traditional prayers for Ramadan at the Anwar Grand Mosque in Addis Ababa.

PILGRIMAGE TO THE TOMB OF SHEIKH HUSSEIN

Twice a year, thousands of Oromos converge at a site in the eastern foothills of the Bale Mountains to honor the thirteenth-century Muslim saint Sheikh Hussein. The first pilgrimage occurs from February to March to commemorate Sheikh Hussein's death; the second occurs from August to September to celebrate the anniversary of the Prophet Muhammad's birth. Each lasts approximately two weeks. Of the approximately fifty thousand Oromos who participate in each pilgrimage, some will make the journey only once in their lives; others will return again and again.

Sheikh Hussein was an Islamic missionary from the Red Sea coast who spread Islam in the Ethiopian interior in the thirteenth century and won many converts and even more admirers. To keep the memory of Sheikh Hussein alive, his followers built a shrine in his honor in a town that bears his name. Originally, only Muslims made the pilgrimage to Sheikh Hussein's tomb. But as the saint's teachings became more widely known over the centuries, other Oromos, who had not yet converted to Islam, began to join the pilgrimage. Those Oromos who undertake the pilgrimage today tend to blend Islam with traditional beliefs. Some of the pilgrims are devout Muslims, while others possess only a nominal faith.

Pilgrims come from all over the country to participate in the sacred journey, some traveling from hundreds of miles away. Many people proceed to the shrine on foot; others ride mules, donkeys, or horses. During the journey—which can sometimes take months to complete—pilgrims are not allowed to cut their hair or sleep indoors. They traditionally carry forked walking sticks known as Oule Sheikh Hussein (OO-lay shake hoo-SANE) as they make their way to the holy site.

Once they arrive at the shrine, the pilgrims take turns entering Sheikh Hussein's tomb by crawling through a small doorway. What follows is an experience filled with mysticism and spiritual power. While believers file inside the tomb, others remain outside to recite poetry, dance, and pray together. All of them hope that by visiting Sheikh Hussein's shrine, they will have both honored the memory of a great man and absorbed some of his ample goodness.

(4) fasting during the month of Ramadan; and (5) making a pilgrimage to Mecca, which is regarded by Muslims to be the holiest city in the world.

Islam first spread to Ethiopia from the Arabian Peninsula in the seventh century. Itinerant Muslim clerics from Arabia introduced their religion to the people along the coast first and then spread farther inland. These clerics initially spread their faith by encouraging Ethiopians to adapt Islam to their way of life, and the strategy bore fruit. By the tenth century, Islam was being adopted by the Afar people of the Denakil region. Eventually the ancient city of Harer became the center of Islamic culture in Ethiopia. Now home to more than ninety mosques and shrines, Harer was periodically used as a base from which the Muslims waged a series of holy wars against the Christian monarchy in the Ethiopian highlands.

Relations between Ethiopia's imperial rulers and the region's Muslim population varied from outright warfare to mutual coexistence. Haile Selassie's government allowed Islamic courts to operate but discouraged the formation of Islamic schools. It did little to promote the teaching of Arabic, the religion's main language. When the Mengistu regime took power in the mid-1970s, it declared some Muslim holy days to be national holidays in an effort to promote greater religious freedom.

The most highly Islamicized ethnic group in Ethiopia today are the Somali; other Muslim peoples include the Afar and the Hareri. Significant numbers of the Oromo, Sidama, and Gurage populations practice Islam as well. Like their Christian neighbors, many Ethiopian Muslims blend their traditional beliefs with the precepts of the religion. Although the degree to which Ethiopians dilute Islam varies, their faith always revolves around the Sunni rather than the Shia branch of Islam.

TRADITIONAL BELIEFS

Traditional belief systems differ from Islam and Christianity in important ways. For example, such belief systems do not revolve around sacred texts or holy books but are based on a set of accumulated values that has been passed down from generation to generation. Traditional belief systems also tend to incorporate a wide variety of gods and spirits, unlike either Islam or Christianity. The exact form that traditional beliefs take depend on the specific ethnic group in question.

Most people adhering to traditional beliefs have faith in a supreme God who is remote, but all-powerful. Spirits usually serve as intermediaries between people and the supreme God. Such spirits often take the form of natural phenomena such as mountains, water, caves, and trees. Some Ethiopians believe in protective spirits, known as *adbar* (AHD-bar) spirits, which are thought to govern the fortunes of communities. The female adbar is believed to offer protection against disease, poverty, and general misfortune, while the male adbar protects against war, conflict, and poor harvests. Evil spirits exist as well. In order to protect themselves against the evil *buda* (BOO-dah) spirit, some Ethiopians wear protective jewelry or call upon the services of specialized clergy known as *debtera* or a local wizard. Spirit mediums are individuals who are perceived to have special powers to communicate with spirits and departed ancestors.

ETHIOPIA'S JEWS

Unlike other nations on the African continent, Ethiopia is home to an indigenous Jewish community, known as the Beta Israel people or the Falashas, which some consider a derogatory term. Of the handful of Jews who remain in Ethiopia today, most live near Lake Tana and in the highlands north of Gonder. The men commonly work as blacksmiths, weavers, and tanners, while the women are known for their skills in making pottery and baskets. These manual trades have traditionally been looked down upon by Amhara Christians. Beta Israel people can often be found living in the same villages as Amharas, but in separate neighborhoods.

Like other Jews, the Beta Israel believe in one God, observe the Sabbath and most Jewish holidays, and circumcise their male children. They also follow strict laws concerning cleanliness and purity, such as that forbidding them from eating animals slaughtered by a non-Jew. Their holy book is the Torah, which is written in Ge'ez, not Hebrew. They do not use the Talmud, because this text was not codified until after the Jews had established themselves in Ethiopia.

Certain references in the Bible refer to black people as "Ethiopians." For Africans in the New World, who had been forced from their homeland into slavery in the Americas and converted to Christianity, or raised as Christians in later generations, these passages held—and for many people today, still hold—particular meaning. They harken back to a time of great African empires, and suggest that black peoples have a proud and deep cultural heritage that predates European civilization. A passage from Psalm 68:31 holds particular importance. It prophesies that "Princes shall come out of Egypt and Ethiopia shall soon stretch out her hands unto God." For people who had been stripped of their heritage, this reference held a promise of liberation and salvation that came to be called Ethiopianism. This spiritual, cultural, and political ideology united African peoples in America and the Caribbean.

The interpretation of these texts took various forms. In Jamaica, the Rastafari movement was born in the 1930s, following the coronation of Ras Tafari Makonnen as the emperor of Ethiopia (right). He became Haile Selassie. Followers of the movement see Haile Selassie as a manifestation of God. More specifically, he is Jah, *the Messiah, the second coming of Jesus Christ, and the fulfillment of the Psalm 68:31 prophesy. During his lifetime, Haile Selassie rejected his own deification, but the belief persists among many Rastafari. Others, however, see him now as an African prophet. Either way, he is revered and worshipped by the faithful, who also view Ethiopia as the Promised Land.*

Today, the Rastafari claim about one million adherents worldwide. The Rastafari culture is associated with reggae music, dreadlock hairstyles, and marijuana, but of course is far more complicated than that. Curiously, the movement never took hold in Ethiopia itself. There are, however, small communities of Jamaicans who have settled there, bringing their culture and religion with them.

The Beta Israel people claim to be descendants of the first Israelites who accompanied Menelik I from Jerusalem to Ethiopia in the tenth century BCE. Although this is difficult to verify, Ethiopian Jews do go back at least to the kingdom of Axum. From the thirteenth century onward, the Ethiopian monarchy waged sporadic wars against the Jewish community. In this century the people have been victims of poverty and discrimination. Their numbers have declined steadily over the years due to war, emigration, famine, and poverty. In the early seventeenth century, approximately half a million Jews lived in Ethiopia; by 1984, fewer than thirty thousand remained.

It was against this background that Israel intervened to offer the Beta Israel a new home. From 1984 to 1985, Israeli troops secretly airlifted eight thousand to thirteen thousand Ethiopian Jews to Israel from refugee camps in Sudan to escape famine and warfare. In May 1991, Israel airlifted fourteen thousand more Ethiopians to Israel. Similar operations continued through 2013, and might be started up again.

INTERNET LINKS

forward.com/culture/181857/the-last-jews-of-ethiopia
This is an article about the Beta Israel people of Ethiopia.

www.oikoumene.org/en/member-churches/ethiopian-orthodox-tewahedo-church
This World Council of Churches page gives an overview of the Ethiopian Orthodox Tewahedo Church.

smithsonianeducation.org/migrations/rasta/rasessay.html
This site presents the informative essay, "Dread History: The African Diaspora, Ethiopianism, and Rastafari."

www.vanityfair.com/news/politics/2014/02/shashemane-ethiopia-rastafarian-utopia
This article, "The Promised Land," highlights a Rastafari community in Ethiopia.

LANGUAGE

Men sit on steps and read newspapers in Addis Ababa.

9

AMHARIC IS ETHIOPIA'S OFFICIAL national language, but only about 29 percent of the people speak it as their primary tongue. A slightly larger number—34 percent—speak Oromo. All of the country's other many languages are spoken by less than 10 percent of the population, and many by less than 1 or 2 percent.

Diversity characterizes almost every aspect of Ethiopian society. Language is no exception. With more than eighty languages and over two hundred dialects spoken within its borders, Ethiopia is, like many other countries on the African continent, a source of fascination to linguists. Amharic was once used for primary school instruction throughout the country, but since 1991 has been replaced in many areas by local languages. English is the most common foreign language and is taught in all secondary schools. Given Ethiopia's linguistic complexity, the ability to speak more than one language is often a necessity. It is not surprising, then, that many Ethiopians are bilingual or multilingual.

Ethiopia's major languages belong to what linguists call the Afroasiatic family of languages. Afroasiatic languages spoken in Ethiopia are categorized into the Semitic, Cushitic, and Omotic groups. Approximately twelve Semitic languages are found in the country, including Amharic, Tigrinya, and Ge'ez (also called Ethiopic). Semitic languages are a branch of the Afroasiatic language family that originates in the Middle East. Arabic and Hebrew are examples of other

Besides speaking their mother tongue, many Ethiopians can communicate in Amharic and English. Although English is not commonly spoken as a mother tongue, it is the medium of instruction in high school and university. It plays an important role in commerce, government, and international communication.

Semitic languages. Cushitic languages, of which there are approximately twenty-two in Ethiopia, include Oromo, Sidama, and Somali. Among the eighteen or so Omotic languages spoken are Welayta and Kefa.

The other major language family found in Ethiopia is Nilo-Saharan. This language family, spoken by only 2 percent of Ethiopia's people, includes East Sudanic, Koman, Berta, and Kunama. Most of Ethiopia's Nilo-Saharan speakers live in the southwestern portion of the country near the border with Sudan and South Sudan.

AMHARIC

Amharic was the national language of Ethiopia during the imperial era—from the Solomonic dynasty in the thirteenth century to the fall of Emperor Haile Selassie in 1974—and has long been associated with courtly life and government. Its use by Ethiopian monarchs earned it the title *Lesane Negest*, which means "language of kings." Derived from the ancient Ge'ez language in the Middle Ages, written Amharic became the official language of imperial correspondence during the reigns of Tewodros II and Yohannes IV in the nineteenth century. Besides being the primary language of government and commerce, Amharic also served as the medium of instruction in Ethiopian primary schools until 1991.

Amharic has a more highly developed written tradition than most other languages used in Ethiopia. It is written left to right using Amharic Fidel, a script, or writing system, in which consonant—vowel sequences are written as a unit. There is no one accepted way to write Amharic using the Roman alphabet.

The Bible was first translated into Amharic in the early nineteenth century. Amharic writing became more widespread by the early twentieth century after Menelik II imported a printing press from Europe. Today, Amharic is spoken by twenty-five million of the country's population as a first language. Between seven to fifteen million speak it as a second language. Although Amharic is still the official language of Ethiopia, it is no longer promoted as the language of national unity as the FDRE recognizes the right of all peoples to use their own working languages. However, Amharic is still considered one of the country's most important means of communication. Amharic continues to play an important role in Addis Ababa. Studies have shown that native Amharic speakers have more education, better literacy skills, and greater employment rates in administrative and professional positions compared to non-Amharic speakers.

GE'EZ

Known as the classical language of Ethiopia, Ge'ez was brought to the Horn of Africa by Semitic peoples

An Orthodox priest at a monastery in Tigray displays a thirteenth-century book handwritten in the ancient language of Ge'ez.

between 2000 BCE and the beginning of the Christian era. Written Ge'ez first appeared around the fourth century CE. Although it was Ethiopia's most important language for centuries, spoken Ge'ez was eventually displaced by Amharic around the sixteenth century. In the Middle Ages, priests and monks translated Greek, Hebrew, and Arabic literary works into Ge'ez. The majority of these early texts dealt with theology, philosophy, law, and history. Perhaps the most famous Ge'ez text is entitled *Kibre Negest*, which means "glory of kings." Written in the fourteenth century by Tigrayan priests, it chronicles and celebrates the reigns of early Ethiopian monarchs.

Although Ge'ez is no longer used in everyday spoken communication, it still finds a place in religious and educational settings. It is studied in some schools as a classical language. Ge'ez is still used as a liturgical language by the Ethiopian Orthodox Church and is occasionally the language of choice for contemporary Ethiopian poets.

The indigenous Ethiopian languages of Ge'ez, Amharic, and Tigrinya are written using a unique set of characters derived from an ancient writing system of South Arabia that

used the Himyaritic alphabet. Ethiopian script contains thirty-one core characters that can be combined in various ways to form almost two hundred more written characters. Since many characters in Ethiopia's writing system represent consonant-vowel combinations, and thus form syllables, Ethiopian script is said to have a syllabary rather than an alphabet. The complexity of Ethiopia's writing system makes learning to read and write more difficult than it is in English. It also makes keyboard typing rather challenging!

Other writing systems are also used in Ethiopia. Arabic script is found in Ethiopia and is used not only for Arabic writing, but occasionally for Hareri and Tigrinya as well. The Roman alphabet is used for writing English and other European languages. Its characters can also be used to write Ethiopian languages. In fact, Ethiopia's new government has encouraged the printing and publishing of written material in the Roman alphabet rather than the traditional Ethiopian script. A setback to this move is the high costs involved in republishing books from traditional Ethiopian script to the Roman alphabet, especially for primary schools, where about twenty local languages are used as the medium of instruction. Ethiopia's printing houses are also too small and inadequately equipped to ensure the success of the government's plan to publish written materials in the Roman alphabet on a large scale.

THE CHALLENGES OF DIVERSITY

Ethiopia's multiplicity of languages has always made achieving national unity a challenge for the country's rulers. In the past the imperial government sought to promote such unity by mandating that Amharic be used as the primary language in Ethiopian schools, newspapers, and on radio and television. This policy sometimes caused non-Amharic speakers to feel discriminated against. When the Mengistu regime came to power in the 1970s it brought non-Amharic languages such as Oromo, Tigrinya, and Somali into radio broadcasts and literacy projects, but Amharic remained the language of government.

The current government is promoting the use of non-Amharic languages in keeping with its program of ethnic self-determination. The country's new administrative regions are largely organized on ethno-linguistic grounds. For example, the Tigray, Afar, Somali, and Oromo regions have declared their predominant languages to be the languages of regional government. This is the case even though their populations are not uniformly speakers of the main language. Some of the smaller regions in the southwest have opted to continue using Amharic. The question many Ethiopians are asking is this: Will the increased use of regional languages other than Amharic promote loyalty to the new federal government or will it encourage ethnic separatism? The answer is not yet clear.

INTERNET LINKS

allafrica.com/stories/201503092412.html
This interesting article examines the role of the English language in Ethiopia.

www.omniglot.com/writing/amharic.htm
Omniglot offers an introduction to Amharic, including the written script and audio recordings.

ARTS

An Ethiopian boy paints a picture of a rock church in Lalibela.

10

ARTISTIC EXPRESSION IN ETHIOPIA has long been influenced by religious beliefs and practices. The Ethiopian Orthodox Tewado Church, for example, has contributed to the country's painting, architecture, and music for centuries. The icons that decorate Ethiopian illuminated manuscripts and churches of the Middle Ages are widely admired as one of the high points of Christian art. Ethiopian Muslims have a rich architectural tradition of their own. They are also known for crafting splendid pieces of ornate jewelry.

Religion continues to stimulate artistic expression today, but creativity in Ethiopia is not limited to churches, mosques, or sacred places. Secular art forms thrive in the country and are produced by both professional artists and ordinary people. The widespread existence of oral literature, arts and crafts, folk songs, and dances attests to the continued importance of the arts in the Ethiopian countryside today. Arts and crafts popular in Ethiopia include metalwork, leatherwork, basketry, weaving, and pottery. Some artisans use animal horns to make cups, shoehorns, lamps, vases, combs, and carvings.

In 2002, the newly formed African Union adopted Ethiopian poet Tsegaye Gabre-Medhin's lines as its anthem: "All sons and daughters of Africa, flesh of the sun and flesh of the sky, let us make Africa the tree of life."

LITERATURE AND DRAMA

Ethiopia has many stories, folktales, and historical legends that are expressed orally rather than written down. Oral literary traditions are particularly common in southern and western Ethiopia and among ethnic Somalis.

Ethiopia's oldest written literary tradition is classical Ge'ez literature, the major works of which feature mostly religious and historical themes. These themes have also featured prominently in Ethiopian plays. One of Ethiopia's best-known dramatic works is *Oda Oak Oracle* by Ethiopia's poet laureate and playwright Tsegaye Gabre-Medhin. First published in English in 1965, the play dramatizes the conflict between superstition and reason in an Ethiopian setting. Tsegaye Gabre-Medhin died in 2006.

VISUAL ARTS

Much of Ethiopia's early art was created to illustrate religious manuscripts or decorate churches. Many ancient churches seem like art galleries, filled with murals, frescoes, and colorful paintings depicting religious figures and symbols. Other early Ethiopian art was designed to pay tribute to national heroes and leaders. Artists usually painted these figures on wood, canvas, or parchment.

Commercial art began to develop in the twentieth century during the reign of Haile Selassie. One popular piece of art depicts the Queen of Sheba's visit to King Solomon and is drawn in an animated, comic-strip style. Sometimes religious and commercial art can merge, as is evident in the popularity of paintings depicting Saint George, an important figure in Ethiopian Orthodox circles. Artists paint representations of Saint George on sheep and goat skins and then sell them to the public. Some artists paint designs on parchment, which is then used to make lampshades.

Well-known Ethiopian artists include Afewerk Tekle, Zerihun Yetmgeta, Gebre Kristos Desta, Skunder Boghossian, Lulseged Retta, and Wosene Worke Kosrof.

WRITERS OUT OF ETHIOPIA

The Ethiopian Diaspora has produced some extraordinary writers. Here are just a few of today's notable authors.

DINAW MENGESTU, *born in Addis Ababa in 1978, is an Ethiopian-American novelist and writer. His family left Ethiopia during the revolution, when he was only two years old. He grew up in Peoria, Illinois. His first novel,* The Beautiful Things That Heaven Bears *came out in 2007, and tells the story of an Ethiopian immigrant in America.* How to Read the Air, *published in 2010, again follows the lives of young Ethiopian immigrants. It won the Ernest Gaines Award for Literary Excellence in 2012. Mengestu's newest book,* All Our Names, *published in 2015, was named a "best book of the year" by a number of important media, including the* New York Times, *the* Washington Post, *and National Public Radio.*

ABRAHAM VERGHESE's *novel,* Cutting for Stone, *was released in 2009 to great acclaim in the United States and around the world. Born in Addis Ababa in 1955, Verghese is the son of Indian parents, but he considers Ethiopia home. He grew up there, and went on to begin his medical education there, but eventually moved to the United States. Today he is both a doctor and a writer.* Cutting for Stone *takes place in both Addis Ababa and New York City and has made many bestseller lists ever since. Verghese, who is a professor of medicine at Stanford University Medical School, has also written several other well-received books.*

MAAZA MENGISTE *was also born in Addis Ababa (in 1971) and lives now in New York. Her novel,* Beneath the Lion's Gaze, *published in the United States in 2010, has won many esteemed awards and accolades. It opens in Addis Ababa in 1974 on the eve of the revolution. It has been praised as "a transcendent and powerful debut."*

NEGA MEZLEKIA *was born in Jijiga, Ethiopia, in 1958, but has lived in Canada since 1985. His past as an armed rebel in Ethiopia during the regime of Mengistu Haile Mariam makes him fear going home. His memoir,* Notes from the Hyena's Belly: An Ethiopian Boyhood *was published in 2000 and has won numerous awards.*

REBECCA G. HAILE, *born in 1965, is an Ethiopian-American who has lived in the United States since she was eleven. That was when her family was forced into exile from their homeland following the 1974 revolution. Her book,* Held at a Distance: My Rediscovery of Ethiopia, *is a memoir about her return to her native country twenty-five years later.*

CHALLENGES FACING WOMEN ARTISTS

For centuries Ethiopian women have been expected to be wives and mothers first and forgo work beyond the household. Even today a woman's employment options outside of the home are limited. Due to family responsibilities and financial hardship, formal female education has been deemphasized, so women have been prevented from competing in spheres dominated by men, such as government and business. The same is true for professional art.

The number of Ethiopian women artists is still relatively small. Women make up only a small proportion of students at the University School of Fine Art and Design in Addis Ababa, and are underrepresented in national exhibitions. Some aspiring female artists apply to study overseas, but find scholarships hard to come by.

Most of the women artists working professionally in Ethiopia today received their training at the University School of Fine Art and Design. Some work as illustrators for newspapers, while others work at the University School or teach art in the primary and secondary schools.

Desta Hagos is one of the most prominent female artists in Ethiopia today. She has displayed her paintings at a number of solo exhibitions. Trained at the University School of Fine Art and Design in the 1960s, Desta is best known for her paintings depicting the natural environment.

The artwork produced by Ethiopian women comes in a variety of styles and genres. Many artists paint scenes of women at work: baking, grinding grain, weaving cloth, or carrying firewood or heavy water jugs. In these works, the message conveyed about the hard life of Ethiopian women is unmistakable. Women artists are also known for painting portraits and nature scenes. Their works vary from realistic to abstract, somber to upbeat. Painting is perhaps the most common art form (in watercolors and oil), but women also produce woodcuts, sketches, collages, sculptures, and tapestries. Despite considerable obstacles, women artists in Ethiopia remain determined to express themselves and to create.

ARTS AND CRAFTS

A large proportion of Ethiopian metalwork springs from the country's religious traditions. Ethiopian Muslims have earned a reputation for producing lovely silver work with geometric patterns and designs that are typical of Islamic art. Most common are decorative pieces of jewelry, such as bracelets, pins, and charm boxes. Metalwork is also prized among the Oromo ethnic group. Oromo women enjoy wearing silver necklaces on which they fasten old European coins for decoration.

Leatherwork is another thriving handicraft industry in Ethiopia because of the country's ample supply of livestock. Belts, bags, and sandals are among the most common items produced and sold. The Afar people use leather to make curved sheaths for their knives; people in the Bale region are known for making fine leather saddles. The *agilgil* (ah-GEHL-gil) is a popular handicraft

Metal objects in a blacksmith's workshop in Axum display complex designs.

that combines leatherwork with basketry. Found among highland societies, this item is a special leather-covered basket used to carry food.

Basketry thrives in many areas of Ethiopia but is particularly well established in Harer. Skilled artisans use local grasses to make baskets and often decorate the finished product with colorful designs. The *mesob* (meh-SOHB) is probably the largest type of basket produced in the country; it often serves as a table in Ethiopian homes and can be seen in Ethiopian restaurants around the world. Like baskets, woven items are also produced for domestic use and find their way into local markets. Heavy blankets, light cotton cloth, woolen caps, and rugs are among the most common woven goods. Pottery is also another of Ethiopia's crafts. Household goods such as jars, dishes, bowls, cooking pots, and water jugs are needed for their practical value, while flowerpots, planters, and ashtrays are produced for the tourist market.

SONG AND DANCE

Ethiopian music reflects both African and Middle Eastern influences but retains a character of its own. Early music was highly religious in character. One of the first known Ethiopian composers was Saint Yared, a sixth-century musician who wrote songs for the Ethiopian Orthodox Church. Today musical chants still form an important part of church services in the Ethiopian Orthodox Church, and religious schools offer training to students wishing to study church hymns, dances, and chants.

Folk music remains very much a part of life in the Ethiopian countryside. Ethiopian minstrels, known locally as *azmari* (az-MAHR-ee), help villagers mark important events by performing at weddings, festivals, and funerals. These minstrels play traditional instruments and act as a catalyst for community participation in musical performances. Although Ethiopia's many ethnic groups have developed their own distinctive styles of song and dance, some kinds of music are common to a number of groups. Folk songs are a common vehicle for expressing political sentiments.

There are a number of musical instruments unique to Ethiopia that give folk music there its distinctive sound. Stringed instruments include two kinds of harps, the *bagana* (beh-geh-NAH) and the *kerar* (kuh-RAHR), and a

USING THE BODY AS A CANVAS

What happens when art, fashion, and tremendous creativity are combined? Among the Surma people, the answer is body painting. Based in the mountains of southwestern Ethiopia, the Surma are a seminomadic people who raise cattle and grow crops for a living. Surma men are known for conducting fierce stick-fighting competitions, while the women are renowned for adorning themselves with lip plates. The Surma's rich tradition of body painting, however, may be their most fascinating custom of all.

The Surma's prime body painting season comes after the October harvest, when people have sufficient leisure time to devote to their art. No one is left out; men and women, young and old, are encouraged to paint and be painted. Before a person is

painted, their body is covered with a mixture of chalk and water. Patterns are then created by someone who removes part of the chalky mixture with their fingertips. The only limit to the designs is in the painter's imagination. Patterns can be vertical, horizontal, diagonal, circular, or any combination thereof. Some patterns are designed to attract the opposite sex, while others might be used to scare away potential enemies. Paintings on the face can resemble a mask or a series of multicolored stars. Surma children have been known to paint one another as if they were twins.

The Surma are not the only Ethiopian people to use body painting as a form of adornment. The Karo of the lower Omo River region also paint one another. Sometimes they paint multicolored, masklike patterns on their faces or patterns that imitate the spots of the guinea fowl.

fiddle-like instrument known as the *masenko* (mah-SEEN-koh). The *meleket* (MAH-leh-ket) is a wooden wind instrument, and the *washint* (WAH-shint) is a bamboo flute. The most common percussion instruments are the *kebero* (KEH-beh-roh), a rattle, and the *atamo* (ah-TAH-moh), a drum. Some popular Ethiopian singers are Aster Aweke, known as Africa's Aretha Franklin, and traditional folk singer Damtew Ayele. Ejigayehu Shibabaw, more popularly known as Gigi, made waves with her 2001 album titled *Gigi* for its exciting fusion of contemporary and traditional music styles. Her second album, *Gold and Wax*, was launched in 2006 to critical acclaim.

Another musician fusing jazz and Latin influences with traditional style is Mulatu Astatke (born 1943), also known as the "Father of Ethiopian Jazz." He blends traditional Ethiopian music with western jazz and plays concerts worldwide. He plays the vibraphone and conga drums, as well as other percussion instruments, keyboards, and organ.

Orthodox Christian devotees carry a traditional drum at the Timkat Festival in January in Addis Ababa.

Although dance in Ethiopia varies by region, it regularly brings members of the opposite sex together for celebration and courtship. The Somalis in the Ogaden engage in special dances following the rainy season. Men wearing white robes serenade eligible women and jump high in the air to show their strength. Women in colorful gowns clap and join in the dancing to the accompaniment of drums. Karo men and women engage in a special seduction dance that often leads to marriage. Men standing in a line jump in unison toward the women, who then come forward to choose their partners.

INTERNET LINKS

www.artistdestahagos.com
The home site for Desta Hagos features her artwork and a biography.

www.cnn.com/2014/09/17/world/africa/mulatu-astatke-spreading-ethio-jazz-world
This excellent article is about musician Mulatu Astake, the creator of Ethio-jazz.

www.inspirationgreen.com/tribes-of-the-omo-valley.html
The body painting art of the Surma and Mursi people is shown here in a series of beautiful photographs.

www.theguardian.com/global-development/booksblog/2015/may/01/best-books-ethiopia-start-your-reading-here
This article reviews three books by Ethiopian authors listed in this chapter.

LEISURE

A skateboarder competes in a local competition in Addis Ababa.

E THIOPIANS LIKE TO PLAY, RELAX, and entertain themselves, but as many people are busy earning a living and making sure that their families are fed, clothed, and housed, they have relatively little time for leisure activities. The country's droughts, famines, and warfare have also seriously eroded people's opportunities to enjoy leisure time.

Children play in a field in Oromia.

11

Abebe Bikila's stunning performance in the marathon at the Rome Olympics in 1960 marked the first time that a gold medal was awarded to a black competitor from sub-Saharan Africa. Coincidentally, that year is considered the year of African independence, because fourteen African nations broke free from European colonial rule.

Boys play foosball outdoors in a park.

Recreational pursuits in Ethiopia do not usually require high-powered technology or expensive equipment. Sporting equipment often needs to be imported and is thus too expensive for the average Ethiopian. Given these circumstances, it is not surprising that soccer and distance running are among Ethiopia's most popular sports. Addis Ababa boasts fine athletic facilities, restaurants, local bars (which the locals call *buna bet*, meaning coffeehouse), movie theaters, and parks, but most rural Ethiopians go without these luxuries.

POPULAR SPORTS

Ethiopia is considered a pioneer of African soccer. The sport was introduced to the country in the 1920s and 1930s, primarily by the Italians. Ethiopians launched their first soccer club, the Saint George Sports Association, in 1935 and established the Ethiopian Football Federation eight years later. After entering international competitions in the late 1940s, Ethiopia launched the African Football Confederation with Egypt and Sudan in 1956. These three nations competed in the first Africa Cup in Khartoum in 1957. Ethiopia celebrated in January 1962, when its national team defeated Egypt 4—2 in

overtime to win the Africa Cup in Addis Ababa. Among the thousands of adoring fans witnessing the great victory was Emperor Haile Selassie.

Today soccer is popular all over Ethiopia. National tournaments are regularly held in Addis Ababa. The Africa Cup competition, which is hosted occasionally by the capital, draws large crowds to the thirty-thousand-seat Addis Ababa Stadium. International soccer matches are broadcast frequently on Ethiopian television and are very popular, especially the World Cup. Ethiopia itself is a regular at the FIFA World Cup qualifiers, entering its first qualifiers match in 1962. Although Ethiopia has never advanced past the competition qualifiers to the final round, it did have its best moment in 1983, when it defeated Djibouti 8—1.

The Olympic Games have attracted many talented Ethiopian athletes, particularly distance runners. The high altitude in many parts of Ethiopia provides an ideal training ground for runners, just as it does in neighboring Kenya, which has also produced world-class runners. Prior to the 2016 Summer Olympics, Ethiopians had won forty-five Olympic medals in total, all in athletics. Athletics, in Olympic terminology, refers to the track and field events of running, walking, jumping, and throwing sports.

Ethiopians also participate in basketball, volleyball, tennis, boxing,

Little boys play soccer in the street with a handmade ball in Gonder.

At the beginning of the 1960 summer games in Rome, Abebe Bikila was a little-known member of Haile Selassie's Imperial Guard. When the games were over, Abebe had become the greatest sports hero Ethiopia had ever known. His first-place finish in the marathon garnered world attention because he had run the streets of Rome barefoot. Not only was he the first person from black Africa to win an Olympic gold medal, Abebe would be the first to win the Olympic marathon twice. He won the 1964 Olympic marathon just six weeks after his appendix was removed; his time set world and Olympic records.

Abebe's Olympic triumphs made him a hero to sports fans all over Africa. He inspired a whole generation of Ethiopian runners, and his name became synonymous with speed and stamina. He died in 1973 at the age of forty-one, seven years after becoming paralyzed in a near-fatal auto accident. His funeral in Addis Ababa drew thousands of fans and admirers.

Abebe Bikila in the 1960 Olympic games

A more recent Olympic hero is the long-distance runner Kenenisa Bekele (born 1982). He's considered one of the greatest male distance runners of all time—an eleven-time world cross-country champion, a three-time Olympic gold medalist on the track, and the world-record holder at 5,000 and 10,000 meters. Kenenisa, who is renowned for his ability to accelerate very quickly at the end of a long distance race, holds many other records, titles, and medals as well. In the 2014 Paris Marathon, for example, he finished in a course record time of 2:05:04.

swimming, and bicycle racing, particularly in urban areas. Most of the competitors in these pastimes, however, are men. Female participation in sports is not as common in Ethiopia—or in Africa as a whole—as it is in the West. Sports have traditionally been viewed as masculine forms of recreation, whereas other leisure pursuits such as singing, visiting friends, or engaging in arts and crafts are less rigidly defined by gender.

SPORTS UNIQUE TO ETHIOPIA

Afar men play a game called *kwosso* (KWOH-soh), a kind of keep-away game in which two teams vie to maintain possession of a goatskin ball. The game is very fast-paced and is played on the hard, sandy desert plain near the Denakil Depression. Sometimes, as many as two hundred men play at one time. Kwosso features frequent tackling and collisions. Injuries occur as players collide and attempt to strip their opponents of the ball. Contestants wear no protective padding and are usually clad only in loincloths because of the intense desert heat. Games can last an entire day.

In *feres gugs* (FAIR-es googs), players on opposing teams mount horses and carry lightweight wooden staffs. Those on offense try to strike the opposing players with their staffs, either by throwing the staffs or by direct contact. Those on defense ward off blows with shields made of hippopotamus or rhinoceros hide and dodge attacks by maneuvering their horses.

GAMES PEOPLE PLAY

Ethiopian adults enjoy games of both skill and chance. Besides cards and chess, Ethiopians play a board game known as *gabata* (geh-beh-TAH). Similar games are played in much of the rest of the continent under different names. In this game, players place seeds in depressions on a wooden game board and then try to capture the seeds of their opponents. Potential moves are governed by complex rules. The player who captures the most seeds wins the game—and often the money that has been bet on the contest beforehand. Gabata is also known as *wari-solo*, *mancala*, or *congkak* in different cultures around the world.

STICK-FIGHTING COMPETITIONS

Stick fighting is one of the most popular sports among the Surma people of southwest Ethiopia. Not only does it test the men's strength, coordination, and competitive zeal, it also serves as a forum through which successful contestants can meet potential wives.

The three-month-long stick-fighting season begins just after the rainy season and pits men from different villages against one another. Duels take place in special clearings with plenty of room for spectators. The contestants, usually unmarried males

between their mid-teens and early thirties, are given 6-foot-long (2 m) wooden poles with which to do battle. Their goal is to knock down their opponents and remain in the game as long as possible, without getting knocked down themselves. Although some competitors are wrapped in protective clothing, others battle in complete nudity to prove their courage. Well-placed blows often hit their mark and cause game-ending injuries. Rules prohibit combatants from killing their opponents; if this occurs, the offending contestant and his family are banished from the village.

Referees officiate in stick-fighting competitions by verifying knockouts and deciding who will qualify for the next round. The field of contestants gradually narrows down to two finalists from an original field as large as fifty. When a winner emerges in the championship round, he is carried on a special platform and gets to choose a bride from a group of young women.

YOUTH RECREATION

One popular form of recreation for Ethiopian children is listening to folktales, which often feature animals as the main characters. A popular theme is the value of generosity over greed.

Children in Ethiopia have invented their own traditional games. *Debebekosh* (deh-BEH-beh-kosh), for example, is the Ethiopian form of hide and seek; *kelelebosh* (keh-LEH-leh-kosh) is Ethiopia's version of jacks. Surma children enjoy participating in the snake dance, in which they squat on the ground and hold onto each other's shoulders, hopping and forming a snakelike pattern on the ground. As they move forward in the slithering procession, the children sing in happy voices.

Youth soccer is popular in both the cities and the countryside. Another sport popular in rural areas is known as *ganna* (gehn-NAH), which resembles field hockey. Urban high schools tend to field teams in volleyball, soccer, gymnastics, and basketball.

INTERNET LINKS

www.bbc.co.uk/nature/humanplanetexplorer/events_and_festivals/stick_fighting
The BBC has a short piece on the stick-fighting of the Suri people, with a video.

www.livemint.com/Leisure/BLZHEQ5xznDR731qnUtIeJ/Kenenisa-Bekeles-marathon-dreams.html
This is an article and interview about Kenenisa Bekele's ultimate goal.

www.nytimes.com/2016/05/16/sports/two-hour-marathon-kenenisa-bekele.html?_r=0
This article about the quest for the two-hour marathon includes a good deal of information about Ethiopian runners.

FESTIVALS

In the main square of Addis Ababa, a woman celebrates the anniversary of the fall of the dictator Mengistu Haile Mariam.

12

MOST ETHIOPIAN FESTIVALS ARE religious in character. Many are tied to the Ethiopian Orthodox Church, which holds special services, ceremonies, and processions during the most important Christian holidays. Although Christian holidays dominate the official Ethiopian calendar, other religious groups have special celebrations that are held throughout the year as well. Ethiopian Muslims observe the holy month of Ramadan, during which they fast between daybreak and sundown. Ethiopians holding traditional beliefs celebrate the change of seasons, harvests, and rites of passage such as birthdays and weddings.

Whatever their religious convictions, Ethiopians observe holidays according to a unique calendar. Unlike the Gregorian calendar, which is used almost everywhere in the world, the Julian calendar used in Ethiopia divides the year into thirteen months. The first twelve months have thirty days each, while the thirteenth month has five days, unless it is a leap year, during which it has six. The first day of the Ethiopian year falls on September 11.

May 28 is the celebration of Ethiopian National Day, also called Derg Downfall Day. It commemorates the collapse of the oppressive and murderous Derg military regime and its leader Mengistu Haile Mariam in 1991. The day is a public holiday and citizens enjoy a day off from work or school.

GANNA

Ganna (gehn-NAH), the Ethiopian Christmas, is celebrated on January 7. Church services marking the sacred day often begin as early as 3 a.m. In Addis Ababa, Ganna services are held at the Church of the Nativity and at Trinity Cathedral, where robed priests carrying prayer staffs officiate. They begin by leading hymns and then conduct Mass, assisted by poets, singers, and drummers. After the service ends at approximately 9 a.m., worshippers return home to mark the occasion with special meals. A ball game also called *ganna* is played in the late afternoon and is an essential part of the day's festivities. Resembling field hockey, ganna is played by men and older boys, who compete until nightfall. In the evenings celebrations continue as people exchange gifts and enjoy refreshments.

TIMKAT

Timkat (TIM-keht), also known as the Feast of Epiphany, is the most important religious festival in Ethiopia. The holiday officially falls on January 19, two weeks after the Ethiopian Christmas, and commemorates the baptism of Jesus. Organized celebrations last three days and include processions on Timkat Eve, the commemoration of the baptism of Christ, and the Feast of Saint Michael, an Ethiopian saint. Ethiopian families

Colorfully dressed celebrators observe the Feast of Timkat.

observe Timkat by brewing beer, baking bread, and feasting on lamb. New clothes are brought out and children are given gifts. All of this takes place beneath the clear and sunny skies of the dry season.

Formal Timkat celebrations begin with church-led processions and all-night prayer vigils. On Timkat Eve, priests remove the *tabot* (TAH-boht), a symbol of the Ark of the Covenant, from their churches and carry it in a procession, making sure that it is covered with an ornate cloth at all times. The processions are led by church leaders carrying sacred relics such as Bibles, crosses, and silver canes. In Addis Ababa, the procession ends up at the old race course known as Jan Medha, where an all-night prayer vigil is held. At a special sunrise service the next morning, an elder of the Ethiopian Orthodox Church presides over a ceremony commemorating Christ's baptism. He dips a cross and a burning candle into some water, then sprinkles the liquid onto the crowd of worshippers. The assembled priests then carry their tabots back to their respective churches in another impressive procession. Some white-robed priests chant and dance while carrying their rattles and silver-tipped staffs. They are often joined in the procession by young boys carrying bells or flags.

The events occurring on Timkat day draw thousands of participants and spectators onto the streets. Ceremonies and parades are held all over

January 7 . . . . *Ganna (Christmas)*

January 10 . . . . *Eid al-Adha (end of the Hajj Pilgrimage to Mecca)*

January 19 . . . . *Timkat (Feast of Epiphany)*

March 2 . . . . *Victory of Adwa commemoration*

March/April . . . . *Good Friday and Easter*

April 6 . . . . *Ethiopian Patriots Day*

April 10. . . . . *Mawlid (Birth of the Prophet Muhammad)*

May 1. . . . . *Labor Day*

May 28 . . . . *National Day*

August 21 . . . . *Buhe*

September 11. . . . . . . *Enkutatash (New Year)*

September 27. . . . . . . *Maskal (Finding of the True Cross)*

December 28 . . . . *Kullubi (Feast of Saint Gabriel)*

(date varies) . . . . *Eid al-Fitr (end of fasting month for Ramadan)*

Ethiopia to mark the festive occasion. Shaded by bright parasols, dignitaries and church elders listen to speeches, while others read passages from the Bible before the faithful. The head of the Ethiopian Orthodox Church, the Abun, usually attends Timkat ceremonies in Addis Ababa, wearing colorful robes befitting his position. Church attendants carry Bibles and crosses in the outdoor procession and wear glittering, jewel-covered capes and robes of velvet and satin.

ENKUTATASH

The Ethiopian New Year is celebrated on September 11, at the end of the rainy season. New Year's Day is called *Enkutatash* (en-koo-TAH-tahsh), meaning gift of jewels, to commemorate the Queen of Sheba's return to Ethiopia after visiting King Solomon, upon which she was given precious jewelry. Today the holiday is marked by the lighting of fires on New Year's Eve. The most important celebration is held at Kostete Yohannes Church in the Gonder region. There, three days of prayers, processions, and services mark the advent of the New Year. In Addis Ababa the biggest celebration is held at Raguel Church on Entoto Mountain. The most pious adherents of the Ethiopian Orthodox tradition observe the Feast of Saint John the Baptist; others simply exchange greetings or cards to mark the New Year.

Ethiopians celebrate the Maskal festival in Lalibela.

MASKAL

Both a secular and a religious holiday, Maskal (mehs-KEHL) is held annually on September 27, two weeks after the Ethiopian New Year. The holiday celebrates the coming of spring as well as the discovery of the True Cross of Christ, which is the cross upon which Jesus was crucified. According to legend, the True Cross of Christ was found by Saint Helena, mother of Constantine the Great, in the fourth century. Later, a relic of the True Cross was given to Ethiopia's kings to reward them for protecting Coptic Christians in their country. Maskal has been celebrated in Ethiopia for more than 1,600 years.

Festivities associated with Maskal include dancing, feasting, parades, gun salutes, and the setting of bonfires. In Addis Ababa an elaborate holiday procession goes from Africa Hall and Jubilee Palace to Maskal Square. Approximately one hundred thousand people come to watch the parade each year, which features bands, finely-decorated floats, and the participation of priests, scouts, civic groups, soldiers, and schoolchildren. Some priests wear white turbans and robes, while others are clad in more colorful garb, including bright caps and flowing capes. Many bring with them ornate bronze crosses, sometimes mounted on poles or worn as pendants. Children participate in the parade by singing and dancing to the accompaniment of drums. At sunset, the assembled crowd watches participants throw torches onto a tall bonfire, which burns all night. This ceremony is observed not only in the capital, but in most town squares and village marketplaces throughout the country.

KULLUBI

Kullubi (koo-LOO-bee), one of the most popular festivals, honors Saint Gabriel, a patron saint for many Orthodox Christians. Viewed as a great protector and miracle worker, he is honored with special celebrations all over the country on December 28. Those eager to pay tribute to the saint make a pilgrimage to Saint Gabriel's church in Kullubi, located in the Harer region 40 miles (64 km) from Dire Dawa. Some of the faithful arrive by car; others find seats on buses or trucks; still others ride mules. Many of the pilgrims walk to the site.

Eventually about one hundred thousand people converge on Kullubi. The pilgrims' primary goal while at Kullubi is to make vows and give thanks to Saint Gabriel. Those who can, crowd into the church for Mass; those left outside listen to services broadcast over loudspeakers. Some pilgrims also bring their babies to be baptized. In fact, during the three-day celebration at Kullubi, approximately one thousand babies are baptized, and many are named after the saint their parents have come to honor.

BUHE (BOO-hay) is an Ethiopian Orthodox Christian holiday that commemorates the transfiguration of Jesus on Mount Tabor. It is celebrated in late August, about three weeks before Enkutatash. People burn bundles of branches and groups of boys go from house to house singing "Hoya, Hoye" until they are given handfuls of bread to eat. In the cities, boys who perform at people's doorsteps are given money.

ISLAMIC HOLIDAYS

EID AL-ADHA This festival is celebrated by Muslims on the tenth day of Dhul Hijja, the twelfth and final month of the Islamic calendar. It commemorates the willingness of the Prophet Ibrahim to sacrifice his son Ishmael for Allah.

Eid al-Adha (EED AHL-ad-ah) is celebrated to mark the end of the hajj, which is a pilgrimage to Mecca. Every able-bodied Muslim who can afford the pilgrimage to Mecca is encouraged to do so at least once in his lifetime. Pilgrims to Mecca dress in simple white unhemmed clothing and perform a series of ritualistic acts symbolic of the lives of Ibrahim and his wife, Hajarah. Some of the rituals include circling around the Ka'abah, the House of Allah, in a counterclockwise direction and walking seven times back and forth between the hills of Safa and Marwah.

A short prayer followed by a sermon giving thanks to Allah starts off the celebration of Eid al-Adha. Muslims who can afford to sacrifice domesticated animals such as goats, sheep, or cows are encouraged to do so. The sacrifice, called Qurban (KOOR-bahn), is then equally divided among family members and the needy.

EID AL-FITR The name of this festival means the day that returns often, and it is celebrated during the ninth month of the Islamic calendar. This celebration marks the end of Ramadan, a month when Muslims fast from dawn to dusk. This festival of cheer, like Eid al-Adha, usually begins with devotees attending special prayers and a short sermon performed in mosques, squares, or any available open areas. In Ethiopia these prayer services are usually held in urban centers rather than in smaller towns and villages. After the prayers, Muslims will don new clothes and visit their friends and relatives. Eid al-Fitr (EED AHL-fitr) is a day of forgiveness, brotherhood, piety, and reflection for the grace, strength, and self-control Allah has given followers of the faith during the fasting month.

INTERNET LINKS

www.ethiopiantreasures.co.uk/pages/festival.htm
The Christian Ethiopian festivals are described on this site.

www.timeanddate.com/holidays/ethiopia
This site lists and explains the major public holidays in Ethiopia.

FOOD

Sacks of lentils, beans, and grains are displayed at the Adi Haki market in Mekele.

13

WHEN IT COMES TO FOOD, Ethiopians like it hot and spicy—and eaten by hand. For most meals, diners forgo silverware and use a large, thin flatbread called injera as both plate and serving utensil. The spongy bread absorbs the spicy sauces and acts as a sort of edible spoon, scooping up bites of food.

A typical Ethiopian meal is served on a large round of injera.

"In Ethiopia, food is often looked at through a strong spiritual lens, stronger than anywhere else I know. It's the focal point of weddings, births, and funerals and is a daily ceremony from the preparation of the meal and the washing of hands to the sharing of meals."
—Marcus Samuelsson (b. 1970), Ethiopian-born, Swedish-raised chef and restaurateur

Many herbs and spices are used to give Ethiopian food its fiery flavor, but perhaps the most essential ingredient is *berbere* (ber-BER-ray), a hot pepper sauce common in many traditional dishes. First-time tasters may find foods spiced with berbere truly scorching, but Ethiopians would not think of having a meal without it. Berbere is a particularly important ingredient in *wat* (weht), a type of spicy stew that is the country's most popular dish.

Besides enjoying spicy food, Ethiopians are less prone to take food for granted. Many families struggle to put enough food on the table and are ever conscious of the specters of drought and famine that have taken such a toll in the past. Ethiopia continues to depend on food imports to feed its people.

COOKING, ETHIOPIAN STYLE

Most rural Ethiopians supply their own food, either by growing grains, fruit, or vegetables or by raising chickens, goats, sheep, or cattle. Although Ethiopians in the countryside often go to the market to obtain certain spices or specialty food items, they rarely have the chance to shop in large grocery stores. Such supermarkets exist only in large urban areas such as Addis Ababa. Only small

A woman makes pancakes at a local market in Omo.

numbers of Ethiopians have access to frozen and convenience foods, and relatively few have kitchen appliances such as refrigerators, electric stoves, or toasters. Food preparation is much more time consuming and labor intensive in Ethiopia than it is in the West.

Most cooking is done by women. Rural women probably spend more time on cooking than on any other task. Meal preparation typically involves gathering wood for the cooking fire, grinding grain, pounding and mixing spices, baking, carrying water, washing and cutting vegetables, and much more. Despite the complexity of many of their dishes, Ethiopian women do not typically use written recipes when cooking. Instead, culinary practices are passed from one generation to the next through example and instruction.

WAT'S FOR DINNER?

Ethiopia's national dish is wat, a type of stew with a rich and spicy sauce, which usually contains salt, garlic, ginger, black pepper, cardamom, onion, lemon juice, nutmeg, wine, water, spiced butter, paprika, fenugreek seeds, and berbere. The spiced butter, known as *niter kebbeh* (NIT-er ki-BAY), is used widely as a spread and in cooking. It's made from butter, onions, garlic, ginger, turmeric, cardamom, cinnamon, cloves, and nutmeg, and is an essential ingredient in wat. The most popular form of wat, *dorowat* (DOR-oh weht), contains chicken. However, wat can also contain beef, lamb, fish, or vegetables. Vegetarian wat, based on lentils, beans, or chickpeas, is eaten by members of the Orthodox Church on fasting days.

Alecha (ah-LEH-chah) is a milder stew than wat. It contains chicken or beef, combined with onions, potatoes, carrots, cabbage, green peppers, chilies, garlic, turmeric, ginger, black pepper, and salt.

The most important side dish in Ethiopian meals is injera, a special kind of bread made from teff, an Ethiopian grain. When preparing injera, Ethiopian women first hand-grind teff grain to make flour. Next they make the batter by combining the flour with water and letting the mixture ferment for three or four days. Then they pour the fermented batter in a circular pattern onto a clay griddle over a fire. Cooking only takes a few minutes. The finished product is a thin, pancake-shaped bread with little pits created by fermentation

bubbles. It has a mild, slightly sour taste and a spongy, limp texture. During mealtimes, injera is kept in a covered basket beside the main dish. Diners use the bread to scoop up food and absorb spicy sauces.

As a rule, Ethiopians do not consume nearly as much meat as Westerners. When a meal does call for meat, chicken, beef, or lamb are the most common choices; in the dry lowland regions, people sometimes eat goat or camel meat. *Kitfo* (KIT-foh) is a popular dish made with raw chopped beef and spices. The first step in making kitfo is to sauté onions, green peppers, chilies, ginger, garlic, and cardamom in spiced butter. Once this is done, lemon juice, berbere, salt, and raw beef are added. The finished kitfo can be an appetizer or a main dish and is often served in green peppers or with injera.

Dried beef is commonly eaten in rural areas. The meat is cut into strips, cured with salt, pepper, and berbere, and hung out to dry in a cool place for approximately two weeks. It is then eaten as a snack.

One of Ethiopia's most popular vegetarian meals is *yataklete kilkil* (yah-TAH-kelt KIL-i-kil), a casserole of fresh vegetables flavored with garlic and ginger. It is served as a main dish during Lent and as a side dish at other times of the year. Typical ingredients for yataklete kilkil, besides garlic and ginger, include potatoes, broccoli, carrots, green beans, onions, cauliflower, green pepper, hot chilies, salt, pepper, and scallions. This meal is traditionally served with injera or rice. *Yemiser selatta* (yeh-mis-SIR seh-LAH-tah) is another vegetarian favorite. This is a lentil-based salad with shallots and chilies, commonly served during Lent.

Although injera is the most popular accompaniment to Ethiopian meals, a number of other side dishes are commonly served throughout the country as well. *Dabo kolo* (DAH-boh KOH-loh) is a roasted cookie made with wheat flour, berbere, sugar, and salt. It makes for a crunchy, spicy snack. *Yeshimbra assa* (yeh-shim-BRAH AH-sa) is the name for fish-shaped snacks made

THE SPICE OF LIFE

It would be hard to imagine Ethiopian food without spices. They are an essential ingredient of the country's most popular dish, wat, and give countless other dishes their flavor and heat. Among Ethiopia's most commonly used spices are pepper, garlic, bishop's weed, rue, mint, cloves, cinnamon, turmeric, and nutmeg.

Several of these spices are combined with powerful peppers, herbs, and water to form berbere, the favorite hot sauce of Ethiopians. Berbere is a key ingredient in beef and chicken stews and is used as a dip for raw meat dishes. The exact ingredients used to make berbere form a long list: paprika, red pepper, salt, ginger, onion, garlic, cloves, cinnamon, nutmeg, cardamom, allspice, black pepper, fenugreek, coriander, red wine, water, vegetable oil, cumin, and turmeric. These items are mixed and heated to form a hot, zesty sauce.

from chickpea flour. Ground chickpeas, oil, onions, berbere, salt and pepper are mixed and formed into a paste. They are then molded into fish shapes and fried. For dessert, Ethiopians sometimes serve strawberries; stalks of sugarcane are also chewed as sweet snacks.

BEVERAGES

Ethiopian cups and glasses are usually filled with milk, beer, wine, tea, or coffee. Milk is traditionally a children's beverage and can come from camels, cows, or goats. Ethiopia's own variety of home-brewed beer is known as *tella* (TEH-lah), and can be made from barley, corn, or wheat. *Tej*, the Ethiopian wine, is made from honey and has been served in the country for centuries. It is usually poured from distinctive narrow-necked glass decanters.

ETHIOPIAN COFFEE CEREMONY

One of the most enjoyable experiences at an Ethiopian restaurant is the traditional coffee ceremony during which the coffee is taken through its complete cycle of preparation in front of the guest.

The event usually starts with a woman bringing out washed coffee beans and roasting them in a roasting pan over a small open fire or coal furnace. The pan is not unlike an old-fashioned popcorn roasting pan. It has a long handle to keep the hand away from the heat, and the woman shakes the pan back and forth so that the beans will not burn. When the coffee beans start to pop, the woman will take the roasted beans and walk around the room, filling the room with the smell of freshly roasted coffee.

The roasted coffee is then placed in a mukecha (moo-KE-ch-a), a heavy wooden bowl, and crushed by a wooden or metal stick known as a zenezena (zay-nay-zay-nah) in a rhythmic up and down fashion, much as how a pestle is used to crush spices in a mortar. Most restaurants today use modern coffee grinders for this process. This is to save time, and the use of mechanical grinders does not take away much from the ceremony.

After crushing the roasted coffee beans into powder, it is put into a jabena (jay-BE-na), a traditional pot made out of clay. Water is added and the brew is boiled over an open fire or coal furnace. Once ready, the coffee aroma fills the room, and the coffee preparation process culminates in the guests sipping the first taste of coffee, served in small Chinese cups called cini (si-ni). Ethiopians usually stay for at least a second serving of coffee and sometimes a third.

DINING OUT IN ADDIS ABABA

Addis Ababa's large population, international visitors, and cultural diversity feed a thriving restaurant industry. Besides traditional Ethiopian cuisine, one can find restaurants in the capital specializing in Italian, Indian, and Chinese food. Places to eat out range from street vendors and small snack bars to gourmet restaurants. Bakeries do a good business, too. The international restaurants in the downtown area cater to the city's sizable affluent clientele seeking epicurean delights in stylish settings.

TRADITIONS AND ETIQUETTE

The majority of Ethiopians living in the countryside do not have fixed mealtimes for breakfast, lunch, and dinner. Instead, they may have one or two hot meals per day and eat smaller portions of bread or dried meat as snacks. If breakfast is eaten, items served might include bread, hard-boiled or raw eggs, or porridge. Often only injera will be eaten in the morning. Ethiopians usually eat their main meal in the evening.

Sit-down meals often start with *tej* and bread. When the main course is served, Ethiopians do not usually use forks or spoons to eat. Instead they use injera to scoop up food and absorb the sauces. Letting one's fingers touch either the main dish, such as wat, or one's mouth while eating is considered bad manners.

Ethiopian restaurants have sprung up in many major US cities, making Ethiopian food probably the most widely available type of African cuisine in the United States.

INTERNET LINKS

www.lonelyplanet.com/ethiopia/travel-tips-and-articles/75930
"Ethiopian Food for Beginners" is an excerpt from the Food and Drink chapter of Lonely Planet's guide to Ethiopia and Eritrea.

uncorneredmarket.com/ethiopian-food
This site presents a good overview of Ethiopian cuisine.

DORO WAT (ETHIOPIAN SPICY CHICKEN STEW)

This stew is often called Ethiopia's national dish. It's typically is served on top of injera, along with other Ethiopian side dishes.

4 tablespoons (60 grams) of
   nit'r qibe (Ethiopian spiced
   butter—find a recipe online),
   or butter or olive oil
2 large yellow onions, diced
1 tablespoon (14 g) of fresh
   garlic, minced
2 tablespoons (30 g) of fresh
   ginger, minced
1 teaspoon (4 g) of jalapeño
   pepper, diced (optional)
2 teaspoons (8 g) of berbere
   spice mix (purchase or find recipe online)
1 cup (225 g) of diced or crushed tomatoes
8 chicken thighs, bone-in
4 hard boiled eggs, shelled
1 cup (250 milliliters) of water
salt and pepper to taste

Heat a large pan on medium heat. Add the butter or oil and onions and cook until soft. Add garlic, ginger, jalapeño, and berbere, and stir frequently to prevent sticking. Add the chicken pieces, skin side down, and cook until browned. Add tomatoes and water, bring to a low boil, reduce heat, cover, and simmer for about 30 to 45 minutes. Add more water if necessary to keep moist.

Finally, add boiled eggs and cook on low heat for another 5 minutes.

YEKIK ALICHA
(YELLOW SPLIT PEAS WITH TURMERIC SAUCE)

This stew is typically served on injera flatbread along with other Ethiopian dishes.

1 cup (225 g) of dried yellow split peas, washed

¼ cup (60 mL) of canola or coconut oil

1 ½ medium yellow onions, finely minced

1 ½ tablespoons (21 g) of puréed
  fresh garlic

1 ½ tablespoons (21 g) of puréed
  fresh, peeled ginger

1 teaspoon (4 g) of turmeric

3 cups (750 mL) of water

Salt to taste

Optional garnish:

Thinly sliced jalapenos with seeds

Finely chopped red bell pepper

Place split peas in a medium saucepan. Cover with water and bring to a boil over high heat. Boil 5 minutes. Let the peas sit in the water until ready to use; drain.

In a medium saucepan, heat oil over medium heat. Add onions. Cook, stirring, for about 8 minutes. Add garlic, ginger, and turmeric, cook for 1 minute, then add drained split peas. Cook, while stirring, for 1 minute. Add the water.

Raise heat to high; bring to boil. Reduce to a simmer, stirring occasionally and adding more water if needed, until split peas are very soft and stew is thick and not soupy, about 30 to 45 minutes. Salt to taste.

If desired, serve garnished with jalapeno and red bell pepper. Makes about 3 cups (750 mL).

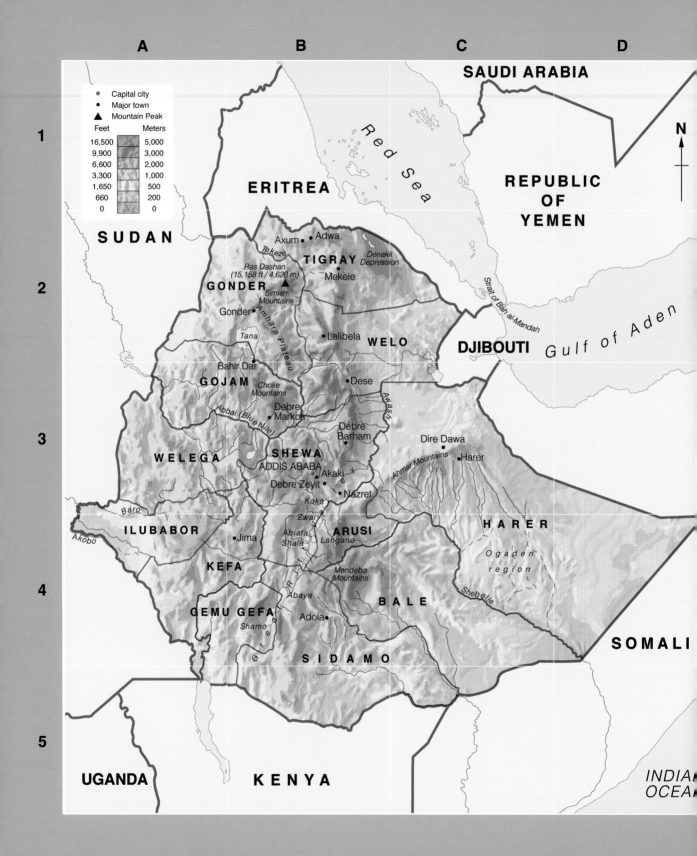

MAP OF ETHIOPIA

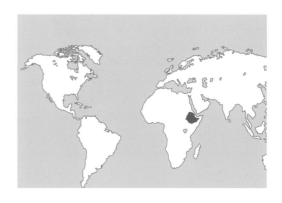

ECONOMIC ETHIOPIA

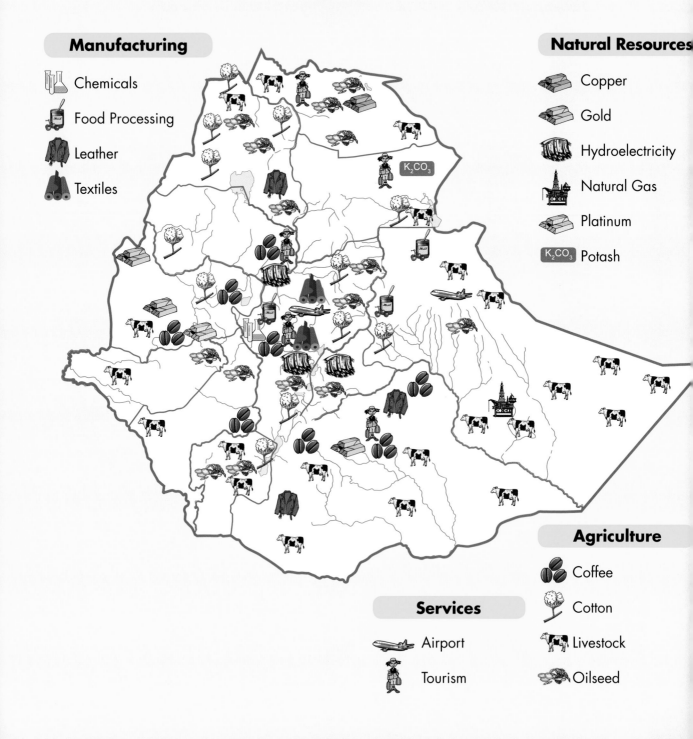

Manufacturing
- Chemicals
- Food Processing
- Leather
- Textiles

Natural Resources
- Copper
- Gold
- Hydroelectricity
- Natural Gas
- Platinum
- K_2CO_3 Potash

Services
- Airport
- Tourism

Agriculture
- Coffee
- Cotton
- Livestock
- Oilseed

ABOUT THE ECONOMY

GROSS DOMESTIC PRODUCT
$70.171 billion (2016 estimate)

GROWTH RATE
8.7 percent (2015)

INFLATION RATE
10.3 percent (2015)

GDP BY SECTOR
Agriculture, 41.4 percent; industry, 15.6 percent; services, 43 percent (2015)

LABOR FORCE
49.27 million (2015)

LABOR FORCE BY OCCUPATION
Agriculture, 85 percent; industry, 5 percent; services, 10 percent (2009)

UNEMPLOYMENT RATE
17.5 percent (2012)

POPULATION BELOW POVERTY LINE
39 percent (2012)

CURRENCY
1 Ethiopian birr (ETB) = 100 cents
Notes: 1; 5; 10; 50; 100 birr
Coins: 1; 5; 10; 25; 50
1 US dollar = 21.55 Ethiopian birr
(USD 1= 21.55 ETB) (May 2016)

NATURAL RESOURCES
Small reserves of gold, platinum, copper, potash, natural gas, hydroelectricity

AGRICULTURAL PRODUCTS
Cereals, coffee, oilseed, cotton, sugarcane, vegetables, khat, cut flowers; hides, cattle, sheep, goats; fish

INDUSTRIAL PRODUCTS
Food processing, beverages, textiles, leather, chemicals, metals processing, cement

MAJOR EXPORTS
Coffee, qat, gold, leather products, live animals, oilseed

MAJOR IMPORTS
Food and live animals, petroleum and petroleum products, chemicals, machinery, motor vehicles, cereals, textiles

MAJOR IMPORT PARTNERS
China 19.2 percent, US 11.4 percent, Saudi Arabia 6.7 percent, India 5 percent (2014)

MAJOR EXPORT PARTNERS
China 17.1 percent, Germany 7.6 percent, US 7.2 percent, Belgium 6.8 percent, Saudi Arabia 6.7 percent (2014)

CULTURAL ETHIOPIA

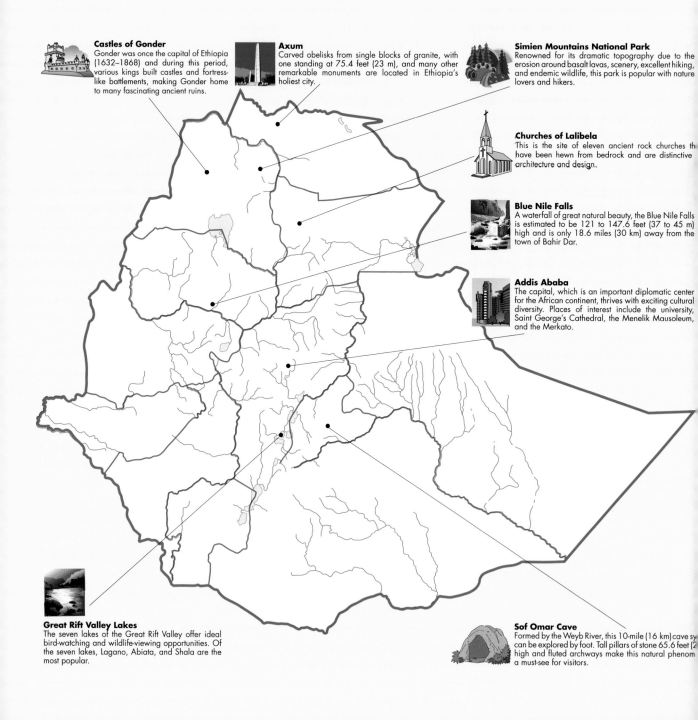

Castles of Gonder
Gonder was once the capital of Ethiopia (1632–1868) and during this period, various kings built castles and fortress-like battlements, making Gonder home to many fascinating ancient ruins.

Axum
Carved obelisks from single blocks of granite, with one standing at 75.4 feet (23 m), and many other remarkable monuments are located in Ethiopia's holiest city.

Simien Mountains National Park
Renowned for its dramatic topography due to the erosion around basalt lavas, scenery, excellent hiking, and endemic wildlife, this park is popular with nature lovers and hikers.

Churches of Lalibela
This is the site of eleven ancient rock churches th have been hewn from bedrock and are distinctive architecture and design.

Blue Nile Falls
A waterfall of great natural beauty, the Blue Nile Falls is estimated to be 121 to 147.6 feet (37 to 45 m) high and is only 18.6 miles (30 km) away from the town of Bahir Dar.

Addis Ababa
The capital, which is an important diplomatic center for the African continent, thrives with exciting cultural diversity. Places of interest include the university, Saint George's Cathedral, the Menelik Mausoleum, and the Merkato.

Great Rift Valley Lakes
The seven lakes of the Great Rift Valley offer ideal bird-watching and wildlife-viewing opportunities. Of the seven lakes, Lagano, Abiata, and Shala are the most popular.

Sof Omar Cave
Formed by the Weyb River, this 10-mile (16 km) cave sy can be explored by foot. Tall pillars of stone 65.6 feet (2 high and fluted archways make this natural phenom a must-see for visitors.

ABOUT THE CULTURE

OFFICIAL NAME
Federal Democratic Republic of Ethiopia

NATIONAL FLAG
Three equal horizontal bands of green, yellow, and red with a yellow pentagram and single yellow rays emanating from the angles between the points on a light blue disk centered on the three bands

CAPITAL
Addis Ababa

AREA
420,000 square miles (1.1 million sq km)

POPULATION
99,465,800 (2015 estimate)

ETHNIC GROUPS
Oromo 34.4 percent, Amhara 27 percent, Somali 6.2 percent, Tigray 6.1 percent, Sidama 4 percent, Gurage 2.5 percent, Welaita 2.3 percent, Hadiya 1.7 percent, Afar 1.7 percent, Gamo 1.5 percent, Gedeo 1.3 percent, Silte 1.3 percent, Kefficho 1.2 percent, other 10.5 percent (2007)

MAJOR RELIGIONS
Ethiopian Orthodox 43.5 percent, Muslim 33.9 percent, Protestant 18.5 percent, traditional 2.7 percent, Catholic 0.7 percent, other 0.6 percent (2007)

MAIN LANGUAGES
Oromo 33.8 percent, Amharic (official national language) 29.3 percent, Somali 6.2 percent, Tigrigna 5.9 percent, Sidamo 4 percent, Wolaytta 2.2 percent, Gurage 2 percent, Afar 1.7 percent, Hadiyya 1.7 percent, Gamo 1.5 percent, Gedeo 1.3 percent, Opuuo 1.2 percent, Kafa 1.1 percent, other 8.1 percent; English, Arabic (2007)

LITERACY RATE
49.1 percent (2015)
Male: 57.2 percent
Female: 41.1 percent

INFANT MORTALITY RATE
53.37 deaths per 1,000 live births (2015)

LIFE EXPECTANCY AT BIRTH
male: 59.11 years
female: 63.93 years (2015)

LEADERS IN POLITICS
Haile Selassie, emperor (1930—1974)
Mengistu Haile Mariam, leader of military government (1977—1991)
Mulatu Teshome (b. 1955 or 1956), president since 2013
Hailemariam Desalegn (b. 1965), prime minister since 2012

TIMELINE

IN ETHIOPIA	IN THE WORLD

5000 BCE
Hunters and gatherers settle in the Ethiopian highlands.

753 BCE
Rome is founded.

116–117 CE
The Roman Empire reaches its greatest extent.

200 CE
Kingdom of Axum becomes a thriving trading center.

330 CE
Christianity declared official religion of Aksumite kingdom.

600 CE
Height of Mayan civilization

1000
The Chinese perfect gunpowder and begin to use it in warfare.

1100–1200
The Zagwe dynasty of monarchs rules over an era of great artistic achievements.

1270
The Solomonic dynasty is restored. The Amharic language and Orthodox Christianity spread throughout the Ethiopian highlands.

1530
Beginning of transatlantic slave trade.

1620
Pilgrims sail the *Mayflower* to America.

1776
US Declaration of Independence

1789–1799
The French Revolution

1861
The US Civil War begins.

1889
Addis Ababa becomes Ethiopia's capital.

1896
Italy invades Ethiopia but is defeated by the Ethiopians at the battle of Adwa.

1914
World War I begins.

1930
Emperor Haile Selassie I coronated.

1936
Emperor Selassie flees Ethiopia. Ethiopia becomes part of Italian East Africa.

1939
World War II begins.

1941
Selassie is restored to the throne when British troops defeat the Italians.